Love
magic

Love magic

LILITH DORSEY

OVER 250 SPELLS AND POTIONS
for Getting It, Keeping It, and Making It Last

**WEISER
BOOKS**

This edition first published in 2016 by Weiser Books,
an imprint of
Red Wheel/Weiser, LLC
With offices at:
65 Parker Street, Suite 7
Newburyport, MA 01950
www.redwheelweiser.com

ISBN: 978-1-57863-592-4

Library of Congress Cataloging-in-Publication Data

Names: Dorsey, Lilith, author.
Title: Love magic : over 250 spells and potions for getting it, keeping it,
  and making it last / Lilith Dorsey.
Description: Newburyport : Weiser Books, 2016.
Identifiers: LCCN 2016042873 | ISBN 9781578635924 (5 x 7 tp : alk. paper)
Subjects: LCSH: Love--Miscellanea. | Magic.
Classification: LCC BF1623.L6 D67 2016 | DDC 177/.7--dc23
LC record available at https://lccn.loc.gov/2016042873

Cover design by Jim Warner
Cover image © Jennifer Borton / istock, calligraphy © Nina Fedorova / Shutterstock
Interior photos/images by Shutterstock, Freepik, Vecteezy
stashom/bigstock.com
Interior by Steve Amarillo / Urban Design LLC
Typeset in Adobe Sabon and Google Open Sans

Printed in Canada
MAR

10 9 8 7 6 5 4 3 2 1

Dedication—To all my loves. . . .

∗ CONTENTS ∗

* INTRODUCTION *

The connection between magic and eroticism is an obvious one. They both encompass absolutely every sense. We lose and find ourselves in magic and love, if we are lucky. Love is the emotion behind the creation of life itself.

Magic, like love, can be mysterious in its appearance and manifestation. It can be graced by divine accident or calculated design. In affairs of the heart, many have looked to magic for a little help or assistance in this glorious domain. Herbs, oils, foods, and sacred chants were sought out as medicinal remedies to bolster fertility and potency. They were used as magical concoctions to conjure up divine love and passion.

For decades I have taught lectures on spirituality and led magic rituals for audiences numbering from two to two thousand. I am always sure to include a segment on sacred cleaning. Your mind and your space must be clear to attract the highest good into your life. Cleanliness is also important to the loving atmosphere you are trying to create. Trust me—you don't want to attract anyone or anything that is filthy or unclean. Many spiritual traditions have ways of cleansing as part of their rituals, and these should be part of any magical working.

This book begins by exploring spells for self-love and happiness. These are at the root of your magical success. One of the most important questions I was ever asked during a possession ritual was "What do you want?" The words came from someone taken with the energy of an ancestor spirit, and they made me think. Our minds, bodies, and souls need to be truly in the right place for us to answer this question. Positive intent and visualization are vital components to successful manifestation. Very often when I do consultations for people about love magic and spellcrafting, they are, for lack of a better word, obsessed. It happens. They want what and whom they want, and they want them yesterday. Sometimes what they want is actually what is best for them in the situation, but more often than not, they are choosing a less desirable option because it is comfortable, familiar, or all they think they deserve. I usually recommend people do readings and cleansings first to make sure nothing is standing in the way of the love. Each situation is unique. I have one client who struggles with communication between her partner and herself. Each time she comes to me for a reading, we discover she needs a different tactic for success. Sometimes all it takes is a simple sprinkling of herbs around her phone to get it to ring; other times she needs a more concentrated Simbi communication candle and ritual to bring about her desires. There are many different and unique roads to success. Meditation and self-care are also important before beginning magical workings; techniques and tips for doing this are also detailed in Chapter One.

Love makes us get out of bed in the morning; it makes us smile, dance, and sing to the hills. My young tween witch self would never have found magic if she hadn't been looking for love, and this is the case with many people. I learned what to ask for, and whom and when to ask as well. Over the years I have done hundreds of readings and spells to find and keep love. I often joke that the multiple psychic reading clients I've had over the years always want to know something about love or money. Well, that is how they present the case 90 percent of the time. Sometimes they just need to be willing to take a leap, to step outside their comfort zone to discover something better. Sometimes people just need to see what was there all along, but they hadn't noticed it. Sometimes people need to "get right with the universe." I apologize if that sounds too much like flower-child speak to you, but there truly is a proper path for people to travel that will make things easier for them. Chapter Two is all about romantic spells in the form of baths, oils, candles, recipes, and rituals that will help you take your first blessed steps down this proper path to love.

A lot of people out there are trying to sell and buy love magic. I've been a professional psychic for over two decades and I've seen a lot. I often get interesting messages from people wanting to make their penis bigger or become porn stars. I'd like to say nothing truly surprises me anymore. Hopefully, I've helped many people find what they were looking for in a relationship, in a partner, and in their life. While I am a spiritual practitioner, I am also an anthropologist and did my undergraduate and graduate studies in this field. My training revolved around ancient cultures, goddess religions, and honored ways of connecting to the divine. It is important to me personally and professionally that I share this type of information. Many modern magical texts are lacking in the historical and traditional background of these subjects, and that is sad. Love spells and magics, in reality, go back to ancient civilizations. We would do well to look to the advice that has survived and thrived in the tests of time. Whenever possible, I have included historically based spells for love and romance. Chapter Two is full of successful spells you can craft to bring romantic love from across the ages to your door.

Romance ignites the sparks of sensual pleasure, and Chapter Three is dedicated to passion, sex, and other lusty magics. Here, there are not only spells and formulas to help you get some sex, but also spiritual ways to make sex better on every level. These spells can be used if you are in a monogamous relationship or adapted to a polyamorous one—the choice is yours. Sensual yet simple, the baths, oils, foods, and more included here will light anyone's fire.

There may come a time with all this love and sex going on that you choose to take the plunge and get married, or handfasted, to your love. Chapter Four is full of spells not just for the ceremony but also to get you to that altar. Learn the real meaning behind traditions like ritually binding your hands or jumping the broom, and make your own sacred memories for your special day.

I had a spiritual teacher tell me once that the real mystery of life was birth, and he was right. To create a life through the loving union of two individuals is one of the most, if not the most, sacred and wondrous things anyone can do. Chapter Five is dedicated to spells and potions for fertility. If you and your partner are genuinely struggling in this area, please try out one or more of the formulas in this chapter, along with medical solutions, until you achieve your desires. Divination and connection to the ancestors are also very important in this type of working.

Chapter Six is dedicated to all types of love that aren't romantic or sexual in nature. Here, you will discover spells for universal love and blessings. Blessings for beasts, friends, and your home are included. I often have people looking for healing spells for those around them, and these can be done on every level. One woman even wanted a blessing for her snake to eat to keep it healthy. We prepared some Damballa candles and a wash for the tank, and honored the power of the great serpent to restore the natural order in her pet's life. There are always magical solutions if we look at things creatively.

Every once in a while things can go wrong and love can get bad, make you go mad, or involve people who have become dangerous to know. Chapter Seven involves spells for removing jealousy, getting rid of a lover, or getting one back who has strayed. Many of these border on the questionable domain of interfering with another's will. Please, as always, proceed with caution.

Chapter Eight blends all the spells and formulas together for you into more complex rites that can be performed by one or more people. Here are rites for the sensual on all levels. Feel free to combine what you have learned in this book and elsewhere to craft larger rituals for love and sensuality.

While all of the spells in this book are relatively simple, some of the ingredients are a bit exotic or unusual. Chapter Nine is a detailed look at the ingredients found in these pages. Use this guide to discover more about the magical items you will be using to manifest your desires.

Magically, I am dedicated to many different spiritual traditions, including Santeria, which is more properly known as La Regla Lucumi. In that religious tradition I have been deemed, through divination, to be a daughter of the goddess (Orisha) Oshun. Her domain is that of love, beauty, money, marriage, gold, and the sacred dance. She is intimately acquainted with all facets of love: laughing, crying, seducing, charming, and complaining. A dear friend of mine, who is also a priest in the religion, likes to say that children of Oshun need to go through all different kinds of love to understand how it really works. My experience has certainly mimicked this. I have seen the good, the bad, and the ugly side of love—no offense intended to anyone reading. I understand why someone needs a book like this, and I understand why I need to write one.

There is, however, one thing that needs to be spoken of concerning love spells, and that is ethics. Many people feel that love spells to change someone's romantic feelings are wrong. Like most things in life, this point is debatable and determined by the actual facts in the situation at hand. The spells and recipes included here are designed to bring about love and joy in your life. Could you use them to harm? Probably, but I hope you won't do that—the same way I hope you use a match to light a candle, and not burn down your annoying neighbor's house. As always, proceed with logic and caution in all your magical workings, especially when it comes to love.

What Is a Spell?

It sounds like this should be an easy question, but what is a spell anyway? Magic spells run the gamut from simply lighting a candle to complex incantations, carvings, and components. A spell can be anything magical you do to effect change in your situation. This can be wearing a magical oil on the way to your first date, or placing a fertility jar under your bed to conceive. Modern pagans often use invocations as part of their spells. Some of the spells in this book contain specific invocations, but please feel free to thoughtfully craft or add your own. Invocations can be as simple as "to the Lord and Lady," "In honor of the God and Goddess," or something similar. If you desire, spells can be combined and layered into larger rites and rituals involving one person or even one hundred. Once you set the stage, anything is possible. You will find suggestions for expanding your magic this way in the final chapter of this book.

As a child, I was a huge fan of media representations of witchcraft like *Bewitched* and others. I believed that a good spell involved a twitch of the nose, a puff of smoke, and a rhyming incantation. Over the years of my magical practice, I have discovered that while these things can be effective, intent and focus are the two most important things you can bring to your magical table. Many of the spells here involve specific instructions and ingredients; by all means, try to use these exactly with no substitutions. This will allow you to be the most successful, but you also should do your best to have focused and positive intent (always backed up by divination) to achieve the best results.

Four Simple Rules for Love Spells

You want to be successful, of course. And everything in this book is designed to help you realize the best possible love and sex, but there are still some basic rules that will help you achieve your desired results.

Magic works on the principle of increase: the more spell work you do, the greater your chances of success. If you light a candle and it doesn't seem to be working, try also using a magical bath or burning some incense.

Magic is a sympathetic system. This means that if you want to connect with the energy of a specific person, you need something belonging to that person, or you need to be where that person is located. You may try to connect with someone remotely, but that can be more difficult, especially for beginners.

Things take time and patience. This is the case for the most accomplished practitioner and beginner alike. We all have our own path to walk.

Be careful what you wish for. I can't stress this one enough. I had a friend once who did tattoos in prison. He had to remove every name he ever put on someone . . . makes you think. Sometimes I hear I have a reputation for being a—well, let's just say—"cautious" priestess; I give cautions to my students and my readers because these are powerful forces we are dealing with. I wouldn't hand a machete to someone who had never seen one before without saying, "Hey, that's sharp." That covered, hopefully this book will provide you with solutions and joys of all kinds in matters of love and sex.

A Note about Altars

Many of the love spells in the book tell you to lay our your ritual items on your working altar. Simply put, your altar usually contains representations of all the elements along with your own psychic power items. It is a place where magic will happen. If you have your own altar already set up for magical crafting, please use this as your working altar. Setting one up for spellwork if you don't have one already is an easy task. Just gather the following items:

White cloth made of natural fabric

Earth item (this can be a crystal or some dirt from the crossroads)

Air item (this can be a feather or incense)

Water item (this can be any sacred water you like)

Fire item (this can be your spell candle for the working or just a white tea light)

Personal item (this can be anything that holds spiritual significance for you—statues, animal charms, wands, ribbons, and the like)

If you don't have a permanent site for sacred space, you can keep these things in a small box and bring them out as necessary. If you like, you can decorate the box with runes, veves, astrological symbols, or other magical inscriptions.

Whole books could be written, and have, about different sacred symbols and signs. Basic astrological symbols can be used in these workings by carving your sun sign symbol and that of your partners onto a candle, or you can include your Venus planetary symbol too. Devotees of Norse paths may wish to include a rune symbol in their working; these simple signs are easily reproduced. In Haitian Vodou and New Orleans Voodoo, we use veve symbols. These symbols were originally said to have been left as patterns in the dirt after a rite. Worshipers began to notice and add to the designs they had discovered, evolving them into a complex system of veves that they use to honor and invoke the Lwa, or sacred entities. Some people may even have a personal symbol, like the late, great artist Prince, that they wish to use in these workings; that's a great idea, too. The more personal you make the workings, the more successful you will be.

Everyone loves a good love story, so let's get started on yours. Enjoy these spells; enjoy those you love; savor the precious time, the delightful tastes, and the sacred love you share together and you will truly be blessed.

Love
magic

Chapter One

HAPPINESS AND SELF-LOVE SPELLS

"Magic is believing in yourself, if you can do that, you can make anything happen."

—JOHANN WOLFGANG VON GOETHE

We fall in love using our entire selves. We wrap our minds, bodies, and souls around another and smile. Even though some people have a hard time accepting this idea, the key to finding love lies within ourselves. Simply put, we must get right with ourselves to get right next to one another. We must be sure we are all right in order to move forward with grace and joy. No one can erase the past, but we must try to not let it cloud our future.

In this chapter there are spells and rituals for cleansing, divination, healing, and joy. These things are at the foundation of all that we hope to do, not just with love magic, but with life in general. Feel free to add these spells to your normal routine, and once you get comfortable with them, don't be afraid to try something new. Magic often operates on the premise of increase, with a serious dose of thoroughness and knowledge added on top. If you find that you are having difficulty achieving success with one particular spell working, you can always try another, perform divination or cleansing, or seek alternative help.

Sacred Geometry

In the world of spellcrafting, placement and proximity are the foundations of the process. This is referred to as *sacred geometry*, and its importance cannot be stressed enough. Your magic and your insight will improve if you attune yourself to these forces. Make use of the following correspondences in setting up your working altar, your ritual space, your sacred space, your table, and in any other way you think might help. Sacred geometry incorporates the magic of both the Earth and the stars. I have included some basic correspondences to get you started from Wiccan, Native American, and other spiritual paths.

Wiccan Elemental Correspondences

The element of Earth is most often associated with North, which in love magic rules passion and courage.

The element of Air is most often associated with East, which in love workings is associated with logic and intellect.

The element of Fire is most often associated with South, which in love magic can be associated with sex, sensuality, and fecundity.

The element of Water is most often associated with West, which in love magic is attached to depth and deep love.

The element of Spirit is most often associated with the center or whole; use this in your love magic to help bring all your elements together and to connect them to the divine.

Feng Shui Elemental Correspondences

Feng Shui is the ancient art of sacred placement. A central element is the *Bagua*, which is a tool used to attune the areas of a space to focused energy areas. The elements are categorized as follows:

Fire is represented by South.

Earth is represented by Southwest.

Marsh is represented by West.

Heaven is represented by Northwest.

Water is represented by North.

Mountain is represented by Northeast.

Thunder is represented by East.

Wind is represented by Southeast.

Native American Medicine Wheel Directions

Several Native American tribes utilize a sacred hoop, or medicine wheel, to spiritually represent the four directions. There is some variation between individual groups, but a basic guide follows:

East is represented by the color yellow.

North is represented by the color red.

West is represented by the color black.

South is represented by the color white.

* * * * * *

Everybody Clean Up

Baths and More

Ritual cleaning is one of the most important things you can do for yourself and your home. Some traditions have their own special blessings for cleansing and banishing negativity. Many northern Native Americans use sage and cedar as a blessing. Southern Native Americans have been known to use Palo Santo, copal, and other items.

In La Regla Lucumi, more commonly known as Santeria, the herb rosemary is very often used for cleansings, and devotees also use more traditional cleansing items like laundry "blue" for purification and ammonia to attract blessings of the air. Ironically, many of the companies that are in the business now of selling magical floor washes and baths originally began selling regular household cleaning supplies. If at all possible, try to make your own formulas with the listed ingredients for the best results.

Cleansing Bath Spell

This simple bath can be taken whenever you feel the need to remove negativity from yourself. If possible, use fresh herbs, as they will contain the most potent energy for your spell.

INGREDIENTS:

½ ounce rosemary
½ ounce basil
¼ cup sea salt
¼ cup Florida water
1 gallon spring water

>> Boil rosemary and basil in spring water. Strain and cool. Add the liquid to a bath along with the rest of the ingredients. Sit in the bath for at least 21 minutes while you envision all your difficulties washing away. After you are done, be sure to watch as the water goes down the drain. Dispose of any residual botanicals in the trash.

Bitter Herbs Cleansing Bath

Many elements of the religion La Regla Lucumi are traditional, and others are conditional. Ideally, this bath is taken using all fresh herbs, including the weeds and plants that grow well in your garden or surroundings. Belief states that the Earth will provide you with what you need to stay safe and protected if you just pay attention.

A long time ago at the beginning of my magical career, I remember I found a spell that called for the herb ambrosia to be used in the bath. I searched high and low and did some serious research, only to find out that *ambrosia* is the common Santeria name for what others call *stinkweed*. That only goes to show one man's ambrosia is another's stinkweed. To that end, please add whatever additional herbs or flowers you feel drawn to, or are literally surrounded by in your daily life, to this spell bath.

INGREDIENTS:

1 handful fresh rosemary
1 handful fresh basil
1 handful fresh sage
1 handful additional herbs from your surroundings
1 large glass jar
1 cup spring water
½ cup holy water
cascarilla

≫ Remove leaves from the stems of the plants and place in the jar. Heat spring water in a pan to a simmer and then pour over the herbs. Next, add the holy water. Draw an equal-armed cross on the jar in cascarilla. Leave the jar uncovered on your windowsill overnight where the moon's rays will bless it. Strain the herbs from the liquid, reserving both. The herbs are to be buried in the earth, or if you live in a big city like me, they can also be composted; check your local health food store for information on community composting efforts. The blessed water is now ready to be used for your bath. This ritual bath is best taken on the new moon, as the energies at that time will help to pull any negative influences from your life. Pour the liquid from the jar into a warm bath, and concentrate on the negative energy washing cleanly away from you. This is a good bath to perform before any major ritual or spellworking.

Happiness Bath

Like attracts like. The happier you are, the more likely you are to find and experience more happiness. Use the following bath weekly, monthly, or whenever you just need to feel better.

INGREDIENTS:

½ cup Florida water

½ cup rose water

5 drops lavender oil

5 drops carnation oil

≫ Mix all ingredients together and add to bathwater. Bathe for 10 minutes or longer. Be sure to immerse your hands, feet, and head if possible. Repeat frequently to attract joy into your life, whenever you have had a bad day, or just need a little lift.

Clarity Bath

This ritual bath is designed to bring clarity and insight into your situation. You can use this bath before performing a major divination, or just when you lack direction in a situation. When time and tide muddy the magical waters, this clarity bath can provide relief for beginners and seasoned veterans alike.

INGREDIENTS:

6 drops holy water

6 drops sandalwood oil

6 drops myrrh oil

1 small amethyst crystal

≫ Combine all ingredients in a warm bath. Immerse yourself in the water on the full moon. Repeat monthly or whenever needed.

* * * * * *

Mindfulness and Meditation Magic

Candles and Oils

"Wherever you go, you take yourself with you." There is a homeless man in my neighborhood who wanders around saying this every day. It always brings a smile to my face because it's true. We must know ourselves in order to know and effect change in the world around us.

The importance of being present in one's body cannot be overestimated. This is at the fundamental core of beginning to connect with another. Mindfulness meditation can be a joyful lifelong study and practice. It involves being comfortable feeling the fullness of your entire body. Exploring what you find. Breathing in deeply and remembering to stay fully present in the moment, feeling your breath as it enters your body. Try to remain mindful as you perform the spells in this chapter and throughout the book.

Reality Candle Spell

No, a reality spell isn't one you do while watching reality television. Most of those participants could probably use a healthy dose of reality though. Sometimes in love it is hard to be objective. This candle will help with clarity, direction, and an accurate assessment of love in the specific situation you are facing. Are your partner's feelings genuine? How is this relationship going to proceed? This candle can help you answer those questions.

INGREDIENTS:

3 drops sandalwood oil

3 drops frankincense oil

1 white seven-day candle in glass

>> Place oils on the candle, light, and meditate on your current situation. Spend time with the candle every evening before extinguishing it. Continue until it has burned completely away. Be sure to record any dreams you have during this time, as they may hold extra insight into your situation.

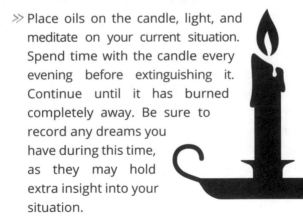

Healthy Start Candle Spell

This candle will help you remove any physical and emotional blockages to love.

INGREDIENTS:

1 white seven-day candle

1 black seven-day candle

12 drops carnation oil

6 drops lavender oil

6 drops bergamot oil

2 pinches dried basil

1 personal item

>> To each candle, add 6 drops carnation oil, 3 drops each of lavender and bergamot oil, and a small pinch of dried basil. This spell is best performed on the new moon. To begin this spell, set up your working altar space with a white cloth. Once you have added your herbs and oils to the candles, place them on the cloth and then place your personal item between the two candles on the altar. Light both candles. Sit for a while as you consider your past and focus on your future. Pay careful attention to how the candles burn. The black candle is representative of the negative forces impacting your life and your situation, and the white represents the new energies that are on the way. Burn for 1–3 hours each night until the candles are finished. Recycle the glass if possible with your local municipality or dispose of in the trash.

Joy Candle

Here is a great candle spell to do anytime. I have a variation of this candle going in my home almost every day. You can't get too much joy! You can simply add a few drops of oils to a tea light or votive candle, or you can use a larger seven-day candle as described here.

INGREDIENTS:

symbol for joy (this could be a veve, rune, or simply the astrological sign for the sun)
1 yellow seven-day pull-out candle
3 drops frangipani oil
3 drops ylang ylang oil
3 drops magnolia oil
3 drops heliotrope oil

≫ Carve your symbol of joy onto the candle using a quill or ritual knife. Add the oils to the candle, which you have placed in the jar. Light, take a deep breath, and enjoy! Repeat as needed!

Am I Blue Meditation Candle

This candle uses some traditional items from both mindfulness practice and other methods of meditation from around the globe. If there are personal scents you also find useful for calm or peace, please add them to this mixture. This formula can be useful in alleviating depression and everyday stress.

INGREDIENTS:

glass candle holder
small amount of spring water
1 blue votive candle
3 drops lotus oil
3 drops basil oil
3 drops rosewood oil

>> Place the candle holder on your working altar. Add a small amount of spring water to the bottom. Place the votive candle in the glass and add the oils. At this time, if you wish, you may recite a mudra or other prayer for peace and spiritual calm. If you have been feeling disconnected or frenzied, light this candle for three consecutive nights to help with the situation.

Peace Oil

Use whenever you are going to meditate or need calm.

INGREDIENTS:

11 drops lavender oil
6 drops lilac oil
6 drops myrrh oil
¼ ounce sweet almond oil
glass bottle
cotton balls

>> Combine oils in a glass bottle. Leave overnight with the bottle covered in cotton balls to charge it with energy and then use the oil when necessary.

Ishtar Oil for Divination

Ishtar is a gatekeeper goddess. Her realms are the mysteries of the divine unknown. In many ways she is a love goddess too, making her a perfect choice for tarot or other psychic investigations concerning love. Some people translate the very name Ishtar, or Innana, as "Queen of the Stars." Consequently, ancient depictions of her often feature moons and stars; you can put these symbols on your oil bottle or other ritual tools, or just reproduce them on a piece of parchment paper and wrap it around the bottle or carry in your pocket.

INGREDIENTS:

3 drops amber paste

3 drops jasmine oil

3 drops frankincense oil

1 drop cinnamon oil

sweet almond oil (for base)

glass bottle

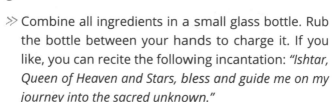

≫ Combine all ingredients in a small glass bottle. Rub the bottle between your hands to charge it. If you like, you can recite the following incantation: *"Ishtar, Queen of Heaven and Stars, bless and guide me on my journey into the sacred unknown."*

Jinx-Removing Oil

Many times when a client comes to me for a reading or love working, sometimes what is in fact the problem is that the person is suffering from a curse or hex. Simply put, this can be negativity from a jealous ex-lover or from the universe. In the end, all that matters is how to get rid of it. (Do not use this formula if pregnant or nursing as rue and sage can be dangerous for you at this time.)

INGREDIENTS:
3 drops pine oil
3 drops sage oil
1 drop rue oil
sweet almond oil for base
glass bottle

>> Combine all ingredients in a small glass bottle. Leave the bottle on the windowsill for a full day so it can become charged with the energy of both the moon and sun. Use daily or until you begin to feel your situation improve.

Road Opener Oil Spell

Sometimes unnecessary things stand in the way of our true success. Maybe you have a difficult situation at work or at home. Maybe there is a person or thing blocking your way. For best results, craft this oil on the full moon and use often. You can also make this into a useful floor wash by mixing with one gallon of spring water.

INGREDIENTS:
1 ounce abre camino oil or cologne
pinch coffee grounds
1 ounce sweet almond oil
3 drops cinnamon oil
glass bottle

>> Combine all ingredients in a glass bottle. Shake well to combine. Use liberally before beginning any serious working, or when you are having difficulties.

Here Be Dragons Protection Oil

This formula uses dragon's blood oil and the energy of dragons to help protect you in all you do.

INGREDIENTS:

¼ ounce dragon's blood oil
3 drops Dittany of Crete oil
¼ ounce sweet almond oil
glass bottle

>> Combine all ingredients in a small glass bottle. Rub between your hands to charge. Wear whenever you feel you need extra protection.

* * * * * *

Heal Thyself, Know Thyself

Healing, Cleansing, and Divination Spells

I recommend divination and healing work to almost everyone who comes to me, regardless of their problem. The spells in this section are to help you on every level to find the perfect path and course of action for you.

Three Roses Healing Spell

This spell combines a rose in solid, liquid, and living form. It will help you heal from old relationships and negative beliefs about love.

INGREDIENTS:
large bowl
1 rose of Jericho
1 cup rose water
1 piece of rose quartz

≫ Take a large bowl and place the rose of Jericho in the center. Pour rose water over. Place the rose quartz in the center. Leave the bowl in the windowsill, where it will be touched by moonbeams. As the rose of Jericho comes back to life, past wounds of

love will begin to heal. Add more water as necessary. After about two weeks, the rose may begin to
decline. Bury it in the Earth when you are done.

Back Away Spell

This spell uses jinx-removing oil; you can use the
recipe presented earlier or purchase a ready-made formula. Use it on the waning moon to help remove all
jinxes, curses, and unwanted and unnecessary influences from your life.

INGREDIENTS:

3 drops jinx-removing oil
3 drops sandalwood oil
1 seven-day reversible candle

≫ Place the oils on the candle and light. Burn for three
consecutive nights during the waning moon, after
which you can dispose of whatever is left in the trash.

Tarot Birthing/ReBirthing Spell

Tarot cards are like any other magical tool. They need
to be charged, blessed, and created (or "birthed") into
existence. There are lots of different ways to do this,
probably as many as there are people who read cards.
This spell, however, is my favorite one, and I have been
recommending it for over a decade. The first thing you
need to do is choose a name for your deck. This process
is similar to naming an animal; it is important to listen

and learn from what you are naming rather than just rushing forward and assigning a character before you discover what is present. Take a few days of sleeping with the deck under your pillow or meditating with it and its energy before choosing a name. Write this name on a small piece of paper. Then get the items together that you will need for the working.

INGREDIENTS OR ITEMS NEEDED:
1 black altar cloth
tarot cards
tarot bag
1 quartz crystal
1 jet or onyx crystal
1 amber resin
1 small purple candle
3 drops myrrh oil

>> Place the altar cloth on a safe and sacred space. Lay the tarot cards, bag, and crystals on the table. Put the candle in a candle holder, add 3 drops of myrrh oil to the candle, and light. Leave the candle to burn with the cards until it is finished. Be sure to keep an eye on it for safety purposes. When the candle is done, put the crystals, name paper, and cards into the tarot bag. You can repeat this with your cards as a rebirthing if desired—just use a new candle. This spell is good to repeat if you have done several readings in a row, or monthly on the night of the full moon as a regular recharging ritual.

Clear My Mind's Eye Gris-Gris Bag Spell

Many times it is hard to have clear vision, as opposed to wishful thinking, in matters of love. I have seen people cry over losing lovers who had no job and bad teeth. This spell will help you gain clarity in matters of love or any situation you are struggling with.

INGREDIENTS:

1 small blue bag, made of natural fabric

6 pinches lavender, dried

6 pinches clary sage, dried

3 pinches myrrh resin

3 pinches frankincense resin

1 small clear quartz crystal

>> Place all the ingredients in the bag. Close the bag tightly and throw it gently in the air and catch it. This gives it the blessing of the invisible world. For best results, wear the bag around your neck or carry it in your pocket.

Chakra Rebalancing Crystal Spell

This is one of the most helpful workings anyone can do. If you haven't tried realigning your chakras this way, I promise you will not be disappointed. You will need some assistance for this spell, however, as it is difficult to place the crystals in the proper locations by yourself.

INGREDIENTS:

2 yards or more of natural white cloth

1 crystal for the Root chakra, or *Muladhara,*
   which rules security and primal energy
   crystals—hematite, onyx

1 crystal for Sacral chakra, or *Svadhisthana,*
   which rules intimacy and sexuality
   crystals—carnelian, ruby

1 crystal for the Solar Plexis chakra, or *Manipura,*
   which rules desire and inner strength
   crystals—amber, citrine, topaz

1 crystal for the Heart chakra, or *Anahata,*
   which rules self-esteem and love
   crystals—moonstone, turquoise, rose quartz

1 crystal for the Throat chakra, or *Vishuddha*, which
  rules speech, creative expression, and individual will
  crystals—blue lace agate, sapphire
1 crystal for the Third Eye chakra, or *Ajna*,
  which rules insight and intuition
  crystals—amethyst, lapis lazuli
1 crystal for the Crown chakra, or *Sahasrara*,
  which rules inspiration and higher consciousness
  crystals—diamond, selenite

≫ Place the white cloth on the floor. Make sure you are
wearing comfortable or loose-fitting clothing; you
can even choose to do this spell working nude, or
skyclad, as the Wiccans say, if you so desire. Lie flat on
the floor. Starting with your Root chakra, have your
helper place the crystal in the proper location. Be sure
to feel and energetically process the stone before
asking your helper to move on to the next chakra.
Once all the stones are in place, feel the full effect on
your body. Breathe deeply. Focus your energy slowly
as you move your attention through your chakras.
Move up from the Root chakra to the Crown chakra
and then back down again. Pay special attention to
any blockages or uncomfortable moments, as they
may hold the keys to some issue. Perform this spell
as often as necessary; it's great to do before any large
ritual or energy working like a massage.

Home Cleansing Spell

This spell should be done monthly on the new moon or whenever you feel the energy in your house is unpleasant. If the home is occupied by a pregnant or nursing mother, please leave out the sage, as this can cause problems. In that case, just use cedar alone.

INGREDIENTS:
bowl of spring water
½ cup Florida water
sage and cedar smudge stick

≫ Place the bowl of water in the center of the home. Add the Florida water. Next, walk around the outside of the home counterclockwise, burning the smudge stick. Concentrate on all the negativity leaving your life and home. When you have completed the circle, place the smudge stick on the ground and go inside the home. Pick up the water bowl, bring it outside, and dump it over the smudge stick. Bury the remains of the smudge stick at the nearest crossroads. Do not look back.

St. Dymphna Sanity Spell

In the Catholic faith, St. Dymphna is the patron saint of the mentally ill. Most people definitely agree love can make you crazy. Hoodoo and other folk magic practitioners often turn to Dymphna in times of distress. She holds a special place for residents of the city of New Orleans, as the International Shrine of St. Jude there contains a famous life-size statue of this saint. Light this candle to receive a calm and sane outlook on things concerning love and family.

INGREDIENTS:
1 blue votive candle
candle holder
image of St. Dymphna
3 drops myrrh oil
3 drops lily oil
Psalm 119 (you may use the King James version here or choose your own; see Appendix A)

≫ Place the candle in its holder on your working altar. Write your name on the back of the image. Place the image of St. Dymphna under the candle holder. Put the oils on top of the candle and light it. Recite Psalm 119 three times. Leave the candle to burn down completely.

Healing and Divination Recipes from the Hearth

Even for the purposes of Love magic, I would say the kitchen is the most important room in the home. I'm not recommending sex in the kitchen because there can be sanitation issues, but to each his own. The kitchen is magical because it is the location of the sacred hearth fire. These days it may just be represented by an electric stove, but the source of vital nourishment comes from there nonetheless.

Beet and Blood Salad

This is a delicious healing ancestor recipe that comes from the Mediterranean. Beets make it a good cleansing recipe for both body and soul. Eat it whenever you are trying to rid yourself of negativity and old baggage.

INGREDIENTS:

6 small purple beets

3 Cara Cara blood oranges

1 tablespoon capers

1 small red onion, sliced thinly

12 black olives, pitted and sliced

1 tablespoon olive oil

2 teaspoons balsamic vinegar

>> Boil beets for 1 hour or until tender. Peel and slice thinly. Place in a large bowl. Peel and slice oranges. Next, add oranges, capers, sliced onion, and olives to bowl. Stir to combine. Add oil and vinegar; mix thoroughly to combine. Chill for one hour or longer. Serves 4–6 people.

Healing Chicken Soup Recipe

Our foremothers knew what they were talking about. It doesn't matter whether you called them Nana, Bubbie, or Grandma; they knew that chicken soup was one of the best magics around for curing what ails you. Some people like to use bone-in chicken and then remove the bones from the soup afterward. Do as you wish, but this recipe calls for deboned chicken, which will save you some time.

INGREDIENTS:
2 pounds chicken parts, deboned
1 cup celery, sliced
1 cup carrots, sliced
1 onion, minced
2 cloves garlic, minced
1 cup mushrooms, sliced
2 quarts water or vegetable stock
pinch of salt and pepper

>> Combine all ingredients in large soup pot. Simmer over low heat for 2–3 hours, adding more water as

necessary if it cooks down. Enjoy whenever you are feeling run down, physically or emotionally, as it will help heal on every level.

Fool's Eggs

I belong to an amazing tarot and spirituality collective of artists called *Esoterico Brooklyn*. We frequently come together for events, and the conversation often turns to food and correspondences with the tarot. This has long been a particular obsession of mine. In tarot, the Fool card is numbered zero; it represents the ultimate turn of the wheel, where everything old is new again. My favorite recipe for saluting this energy is Fool's Eggs. It is great for rituals and situations involving new beginnings.

INGREDIENTS:
12 hard-boiled eggs
¾ cup chipotle mayonnaise
¼ cup pickle relish
1 teaspoon dill
1 teaspoon garlic powder
1 teaspoon chives, minced
salt and pepper to taste
paprika for garnishing

≫ Slice eggs in half and scoop out yolks into a large bowl. Add remaining ingredients. Mix well and add salt and pepper. Spoon filling back into egg whites. Makes 24 halves.

Chapter Two

ROMANCE SPELLS

I saw a tarot deck the other day that featured the image from Disney's *Lady and the Tramp* as the Lovers card. As a child, I remember this story featured heavily in my search to find a tramp at the other end of my spaghetti. As an adult, I keep the memory as a metaphor for connection. Over the years, I have performed many a romantic spell, probably hundreds, for myself and others.

Most romance magic falls into one of two types: the kind where are you are generally asking for the blessing of love and the kind where you are specifically trying to unite individuals. This chapter includes both types of magical spells and formulas. However, the latter type of spell where you are trying to affect specific people is greatly improved by the use of personal items from these people. One of my favorite, and actually true, stories is about a dear friend of mine, Shaughn, who passed away suddenly a few years ago. It fell to me and another close friend of his to sort through his belongings—well, actually, if I'm honest, to remove the porn—before we turned his stuff back over to his family. Sometime after we began, we found what we were looking for in a box marked "art supplies," and we also found something else—a small treasure chest full of women's panties. We laughed out loud. The panties were all different shapes and sizes, and we quickly came to the conclusion that this

was Shaughn's private stash of his romantic magics. As strange as it sounds, underwear—well, clothing in general—is a great item to use to link your working to an individual.

Previously, I spoke about spiritual cleanliness and how the right mind and also body are important when performing any kind of magic. Some people believe that this magical purity extends to celibacy, particularly when it comes to love magic. Then there are some who believe that your sexual power will be increased with the number of sexual encounters or orgasms you have. Clearly, there are two sides to this issue; there are benefits to both methods. My advice if you are considering adopting one of these methods is to examine your magical life so far.

I had a dear friend who was a pioneer in the pagan community and later went on to become a Lucumi priestess. In her "Magic for Beginners" lecture, she would tell people the path to magic should be paved with "difference." By this, she meant to increase your spiritual power, you should start by doing something different. If you always travel home from work or school in the same way, go a different way to help unlock the energies around you. This is some of the best advice I have ever heard. It can be put into practice here as well. If you are someone who is not very sexually adventurous, and you are now trying to become serious about love and sex magic, consider expanding your box—pardon the pun. It may open you up to new experiences. To quote one of my favorite geniuses, Alejandro Jodorowsky: "It is not certain that discipline will give you success, but it is certain that a lack of discipline will give you failure." (Twitter post, April 10, 2015, @alejodorowsky) You can and should apply this discipline wherever it is most necessary in all areas of your life.

Light My Fire Candle Spells

Fire is often responsible for the beginning sparks of love. When I first connected with my partner, in addition to experiencing a divine wave of passion, we also experienced the spontaneous combustion of the ancestor altar closest to us. These candle spells will help you find and foster new love. It goes without saying: keep a fire extinguisher handy!

On Top of You Candle Spell

This spell sounds quite dirty, but basically you are going to write your name over your desired partner's and burn a candle on top of it. You can do this with this particular magical love formula to strengthen your romantic connection, or with any of the other love candle spells listed to give them extra focus.

INGREDIENTS:
parchment paper
dove's blood ink
1 pink seven-day candle in glass

>> Write the full name of your desired partner on a
piece of parchment paper; over that, write your full
name. On top of this, place the seven-day candle
in glass. Burn each night before retiring to bed as
you concentrate on your desired relationship. Be
sure to extinguish the candle by smothering rather
than blowing it out, as this will help contain the energies. Continue the spell until the candle is finished.
Dispose of the remains at the crossroads.

Theia Candle to See Your Love

The ancient Greeks venerated the goddess Theia, who possessed sacred sight and was known for her oracular prowess. Her otherworldly sight was said to be part of the power of the sun. Patrons would make offerings to her and receive a vision of their future love. Light this candle on the new moon to increase your clear vision of love, what it will look like, and how to get there.

INGREDIENTS:

1 yellow or gold seven-day pull-out candle
gold glitter
3 drops sunflower (*Helianthus*) oil
pinch of rose petals
pinch of mugwort
small piece of rose quartz
1 ounce river water

≫ Carve a heart or other sacred symbol for love on your candle. Anoint with oil and then rub with ground rose petal, glitter, and mugwort herbs. Place rose quartz and a small amount of river water in the bottom of the glass. Then place the candle inside the glass. Make the sign of the crossroads in the air with the candle and then light on the full moon. For safety's sake, please never leave a burning candle unattended.

Let Me See Candle

Charromancy is the proper word for divination with candles.

By using a candle and a basin of water, you can attempt to predict how your current or future romance will unfold. Many pagan groups use this method in conjunction with rituals as part of their ceremony. As such, it can be done as a solitary activity or with others.

INGREDIENTS:

red candle in glass

parchment paper

1 cup rose water

1 cup tap water

large white bowl, made of porcelain or glass

>> Light the red candle. On the parchment paper, write down your full birth name and the full name of your lover, if you have one. Concentrate on your desires. After the candle has been burning, carefully pour a small amount of wax into the bowl, filled with the waters. (Remember that wax is hot!) What is the shape you see? Does it resemble a face? A heart? A dragon? Allow yourself to explore the possibilities of what the wax is trying to show you, for herein lies the key to love.

Love Oils

Wearing oils to bring love into your life can remind you of your desires and attract beneficial energies to you throughout the day. Remember especially to wear them before going on a date or actively seeking a potential partner.

Hearts of Dixie Oil

Many love spells come from the hot and sultry southern United States. This one is designed for sweet and courtly love.

INGREDIENTS:
5 drops magnolia oil
5 drops tuberose oil
¼ ounce sweet almond oil
1 small piece vanilla bean

>> It is best to make this oil under the influence of the full moon. Combine all ingredients in a small bottle. Shake to combine.

Sunshine in My Love Oil

When we are lucky, the joys of love feel like sunshine on a warm spring day. The author e. e. cummings said, "lovers alone wear sunlight," and he was blissfully correct. This formula will help bring joyous sunshine to your love life by combining oils ruled by this glorious star.

INGREDIENTS:

5 drops heliotrope oil
5 drops sunflower oil
2 drops cinnamon oil
2 drops frankincense oil
sweet almond oil for base
glass bottle

>> Combine oils together in a glass bottle. For extra energy, you can write the astrological symbol for the sun on the bottle. At noon, leave the bottle outside or on a windowsill where the sun's rays will bless it. After that has been completed, take the sunstruck bottle and rub it between your hands as you envision the joys of love in your life, whatever that looks like for you. Wear the oil daily for best results.

Black Cat Bast Oil

Black cats have a special magic all their own. Their connection to witchcraft has almost become a trope, and many attribute this to the ancient Egyptian goddess Bast. Worship of this deity began around 3500 BCE and included sacred temples and rites to this divine cat, also known as Bastet, Basthet, and Pasch. Hers was a sensual and sacred dance. Wear this oil whenever you wish to honor her energy.

INGREDIENTS:

3 drops sandalwood oil
3 drops myrrh oil
3 drops cypress oil
3 drops lavender oil
¼ ounce sweet almond oil
glass bottle

≫ Combine all ingredients together in a glass bottle. Charge the bottle with your fingertips, rubbing back and forth to infuse it with sacred energy.

Peaceful Path Oil

Dating these days can be a dubious business. I have heard some wild and crazy stories. I even had one friend who had her date get up in the middle of their evening and start to pick up someone else at the bar. People can test our patience sometimes, and it is important to remain calm and dedicated on our true path to love. By the way, my friend kept at it, attended several of my love rituals, and is now happily married with a new baby boy. Make this oil on the full moon and wear it during the start of a new relationship or whenever you need peaceful direction.

INGREDIENTS:
3 drops gardenia oil
3 drops lavender oil
3 drops myrrh oil
3 drops sandalwood oil
½ ounce sweet almond oil
glass bottle

≫ Combine all ingredients in a small glass bottle. Leave on the windowsill overnight for the moon's rays to bless your creation. In the morning, take the bottle and rub it between your hands. Now it is ready for use.

Venus Oil

This love spell is one of the most popular in existence. Venus is a goddess, a planet, a true force to be reckoned with. Use this oil when you are going on a date or looking for a prospective partner.

INGREDIENTS:

5 drops jasmine oil

5 drops rose oil

5 drops amber oil

¼ ounce sweet almond oil

glass bottle

» Combine the ingredients in a glass bottle. Charge with your breath to give it energy.

Freya Friday Oil

In the Norse pantheon, Freya is one of the primary goddesses of love and sensuality. Wear this oil to honor this goddess of springtime and loving abundance.

INGREDIENTS:

2 drops thyme oil

6 drops rose oil

2 drops amber oil

pinch yarrow, dried

pinch gold glitter

¼ ounce sweet almond oil

glass bottle

>> Combine all ingredients together into the glass bottle. Rub the bottle between your hands quickly to charge it. Craft this oil on a Friday, which is said to be Freya's sacred day. If you choose, you may also use an invocation to Freya appropriate to your practice.

Blessed Waters, Baths, and Crystals for Love

Happy Delights Spray

This spray is honestly one of my favorite formulas; I use it daily and carry it with me when I go outside. It creates an energy of loving delight and joy. I use it so often that I even freaked out my partner once when he showed up and the entire room smelled like me. Needless to say, I recommend using this spray often and liberally.

INGREDIENTS:

1 ounce Florida water
1 ounce rose water
3 drops amber oil
1 drop sandalwood oil
1 drop frangipani oil
glass bottle

>> Combine all ingredients into a glass bottle. Make the sign of the cross in the air and throw the bottle gently in the air and catch it. This way, it is blessed by the realm of the invisibles.

Rose Quartz Water

Rose quartz is traditionally a stone of great love and healing. This water spell can be added to a bath, sprinkled about the home, or even placed in a spray bottle and used whenever necessary. This water will help heal your love problems and create an atmosphere of bliss.

INGREDIENTS:

1 cup rose water

1 cup spring water

1 small piece rose quartz crystal

≫ Combine all ingredients on the day of the full moon. Leave the mixture overnight someplace where the moon's rays will touch it. The next morning, it's ready for use.

Oshun Bath

The Santeria goddess of love and beauty, Oshun, blesses this creation. Her sweetness is known to be irresistible. This bath can be used to get your love life flowing in the proper direction.

INGREDIENTS:

2 drops nutmeg oil

3 drops cinnamon oil

5 drops orange oil

½ cup rose water

½ cup river water

≫ Combine all ingredients in the bathtub on the full moon. While you are in the bath, envision Oshun's sensual wisdom and glory washing over you and guiding you toward your loving destiny.

Venus Fountain of Love Bath

Venus, both the goddess and her planet, have been associated with love for aeons. From Botticelli to Warhol, she has been a muse that manifested as a standard of beauty for us all. Use this bath to connect with her great power.

INGREDIENTS:

1 cup spring water
1 small piece of the root from bloodroot
¼ cup mugwort, dried
½ cup red roses, dried
¼ cup thyme, dried
¼ cup yarrow, dried

>> Place spring water in a saucepan over low heat. Add the root and herbs and bring to a simmer. Turn off the heat and let cool. Strain and add to your bath on the full moon to bring the blessing and guidance of Venus.

Satyr Bath

Almost all of the spells and formulas in this book can be done by same-sex or opposite-sex couples. This is one, however, that is designed specifically for gay males; it taps into the energies of Pan, the mischievous horny god of legend.

INGREDIENTS:

3 drops vanilla oil

3 drops pine oil

3 juniper berries

rose water for base

glass bottle

≫ Combine all ingredients in a glass bottle. Sleep with this mixture under your pillow for three nights to charge it with your sexual dreams. Take the bath often with your love as a prelude to loving passion and lusty delights.

Romantic Spells

These spells combine a variety of elements and methods for bringing romance into your life on all levels. Included are a wide variety of folklore spells designed to help you see or prophesy the new love that is coming.

Love Lift Me Crystal Spell

This spell is designed to bring long-lasting romantic love and blessings to your bed.

INGREDIENTS:

2 amethyst crystals

2 rose quartz crystals

1 cup orange flower water

>> Dip the crystals in a large bowl filled with the flower water. Remove the crystals. Dump the water out under a large tree. Place the crystals under the four corners of your bed. Replace monthly or as necessary.

Crossroads of Love Spell

The question of love often leaves people at a spiritual crossroads. Crossroads are known for their magic, a space of in-between where anything can happen. This spell will open you up to new possibilities and help you find your proper direction in love.

INGREDIENTS:

1 antique key
1 cup of coffee
1 red rose
pinch of dirt from the crossroads
glass candle holder
1 red votive candle

>> Go to the crossroads closest to your home. Leave the key, coffee, and red rose. If you like, you can do this at night so you are less likely to be detected. Take a pinch of dirt from the crossroads. Do not look back. When you return to your home, place the pinch of dirt in the bottom of the candle holder, put the candle on top, and light it. New opportunities for love will soon present themselves.

Cowrie Come-On Spell

Ancient Egyptians believed cowrie shells were great magical tools. Other cultures believe that their magic comes from their resemblance to a half-open eye. Still other groups see a similarity between the cowrie and female genitalia, and consequently they have become symbolic of love, passion, and fertility. This spell is designed to bring your true love into your life.

INGREDIENTS:

1 drop rose oil
1 drop sandalwood oil
white tea light candle
5 cowrie shells

>> Lay out the items on your working altar. Place the rose and sandalwood oil on the tea light candle. Arrange the cowrie shells around the candle. Light the candle and meditate on the qualities you want and need in a lover. If you like, you can write these down on a piece of parchment paper. When the candle has burned down, take the cowrie shells to the nearest river. Take four of the shells and your list, if you have one, and throw them into the river, turn around, and do not look back. Take the remaining cowrie shell and keep it in your pocket until your lover makes himself or herself known. Then you may bury the shell at the nearest crossroads.

Visit Your Dreams Astral Travel Spell

Psychic travel between lovers who may not be in the same space physically can be a lovely thing that is sometimes necessary, especially when distance separates you. Many of my former lovers were intrigued and surprised to find me knocking on their dreamtime doors. I highly recommend it. Connecting in this way is much easier when you have a personal item to use to help you; this can be as simple as someone's handwriting.

INGREDIENTS:

tap water

2 glass candle holders

personal item of person you are connecting with

1 pink votive candle

1 white votive candle

>> Place a small amount of tap water (to represent the spirit of place) into each candle holder. Take the personal item and place it safely under one of the candle holders. Into that holder, place the pink candle. Into the other candle holder, add the white candle. Light both candles and meditate on the physical space of your lover. If you have been there, remember yourself in that space. Imagine every possible detail. Meditate on moving in and through that space. This is best done on the night of the full moon. When the candles have burned out, remove the personal item and place it under your bed. This will help you travel during your sleep to the place you desire.

Aphrodite Apple Spell for Love

Aphrodite is the beloved Greek goddess of love. My dear friend, the late, great Isaac Bonewits, had a particular fondness for this lovely lady. For many years, he carried a separate tent to pagan festivals and set it up as a mobile shrine. People would leave offerings of flowers, candles, and food. Shrines for Aphrodite represent her sensual beauty in all forms. Very quickly her power became evident. Everyone who left an offering seemed to have a sexual encounter or receive another blessing of love very quickly. This apple spell is designed to bring speedy love to you and to help the right situation find you quickly and easily.

INGREDIENTS:

1 red apple
6 drops rose oil
6 drops ylang ylang oil
1 small red candle
candle holder
ritual knife or athame for carving

>> Slice the apple in half across the middle to reveal a star pattern. Trace the star pattern onto one of the halves with your ritual blade. Next, carve a heart on top of the star. Repeat to the best of your ability with the other apple half. On each apple half, place

2 drops rose oil and 2 drops ylang ylang oil. Take one apple half and leave this at the crossroads nearest your house. Place it down, turn around, and do not look back. When you return home, take the red candle and place in the candle holder. Put 2 drops of rose oil and 2 drops of ylang ylang oil on the candle. Place on your altar next to the remaining apple half and light. When the candle has burned down, you may dispose of the remaining wax and the apple in the garbage.

Backward and Forward Spell

This ritual spell is designed to refine everything it is you want and don't want in a new partner. It is especially helpful when you have ended a relationship and are seriously ready to find another. This spell will help you focus and refine your efforts.

INGREDIENTS:
1 small notebook
red pen

>> Take the notebook, and from the first page to the center of the book, write everything you want in a partner. Include every detail—physical, emotional, mental, taste in music, everything. Then from the back to the middle, write everything you don't want in a partner—pet peeves, must-haves, everything. Then sleep with this notebook under your bed or

pillow, starting on the full moon. Pay attention to your dreams, as they may provide clues to discovering your new love. Leave the notebook there for one week, or up to a full month if necessary.

St. Ann I Need a Man Hoodoo Request Spell

Hoodoo spells very often make use of whatever materials are available at the time, and are then fueled by the determination and intent of the practitioner. This spell is no different: it requires a bit of patience, a bit of diligence, and a bit of creativity.

INGREDIENTS:
photo or image of St. Ann
1 drop cinnamon oil
1 drop sweet orange oil
3 pennies

» On the back of the image, write all the qualities you want in a partner—good lover, kind, blue eyes . . . whatever it is that lifts your dress, as they say. Anoint the photo with the oils. Go to the nearest church of St. Ann and bury the picture along with the three pennies at the crossroads as close to the church as possible. Say the words *"St. Ann, St. Ann, I need a man (woman). From head to toe, bring him (her) as soon as you can."* After you leave the offering, do not look back.

Big and Little Poppet Spell
to Bring Lovers Together

Using dolls for spellwork, while associated with Voodoo, actually has very different roots. In reality, many Wiccan practitioners employ the use of poppets (or dolls) for symbolic representation, in their romantic love spells. These are commonly filled with a piece of clothing, hair, or other personal item from the individual, along with herbs and other magical items. This spell will help bring you together with the specific person you desire.

INGREDIENTS:

1 cup red rose petals, dried

1 tablespoon nutmeg, ground

3 drops jasmine oil

3 drops ylang ylang oil

3 drops sunflower oil

pink fabric, made of cotton or other natural material

pink or red thread, to sew with

personal items from the two people

>> It is best to start creating these dolls on the eve of the full moon. In a large bowl, add rose petals, nutmeg, and oils. Leave the bowl on a windowsill or outside, where it will be blessed by the moonlight overnight. In the morning, take the bowl and stir the contents clockwise as you visualize your desires. A positive vision is key to the success of this working. When you

feel you have energized your spell, fill the poppets with half the mixture in each. Next, place the personal items into the dolls and sew them up. Now it is time to put them together. You can choose to join the dolls by the hand, head, heart, or all three. Place the dolls together and tie with red or pink thread. If you choose red, the connection will be filled with more lust, and if you choose pink, the focus will be more on romance. Leave the dolls together for as long as the couple is together. This spell has been known to have intense results. Use with caution.

Two of Cups Love Spell

Using tarot cards in your spellwork can be an effective tool for focus and success. The Two of Cups is a card of deep and abiding union, and this spell will help bring that into your life.

INGREDIENTS:

red altar cloth

Two of Cups tarot card (from any deck)

2 cups

1 cup rose water

6 drops rose oil

6 drops orange blossom oil

glass candle holder

1 pink votive candle

2 small pieces rose quartz crystal

≫ Lay your altar cloth out on your space. Place the tarot card in the center. Put one cup on either side of the card. Fill the cups equally with rose water and the crystals. Then to each cup add 2 drops each rose oil and orange blossom oil. Place the candle holder on top of the card and place the pink candle in

Two of Cups

it. Place 2 drops of each oil on the candle and light. When the candle has burned down, remove the two crystals from the cups and dispose of the rest. You and your lover should carry the crystals in your pocket as a magical talisman for your love. This spell is best performed on the full moon.

Simple Folklore Spells to Find Love

• *Lift the Veil Samhain Spell*—For many pagans, Samhain, more commonly known as Halloween, is the time when the doorway between the worlds of the visible and the invisible is open. This spell will help you see your future mate. On the eve of Samhain, walk up and down your street three times carrying a hand mirror. Say these words: *"Sacred mirror that's in front of me, show me my future spouse to be."* Look into the mirror, and a vision of your new love should come to you.

- **Back It Up Mirror Spell**—On the eve of the full moon, just as the sun is setting, walk backward toward your bed carrying a hand mirror. When you get to the bed, sit down and look in the mirror. It is said you will be able to see your future husband or wife.

- **Quench My Thirst Dream Spell**—Take a white egg and start rolling it over your feet, up the sides, then over your body, and around your head. Boil the egg and slice it in half. (*Note:* If the egg in any way looks discolored or bad, throw it away, light a white candle, and start over. Then boil the new egg.) Take one half and leave it at the crossroads nearest your home and don't look back. When you return to your house, take the other half, remove the yolk, and dispose of it. Fill the remaining white with a sprinkle of sea salt. Eat the egg. In your dreams, the person who offers you a glass of water is said to be your future mate.

- **Lusty Month of May Spell**—Just as Samhain (Halloween) holds special significance for pagans, so does Beltane (or May 1). Occupying the exact opposite point on the calendar from Samhain, this time is celebrated as one of increase and joy. A folk magic spell from the Ozarks says to take a mirror out to a well or other body of water on this day. As the sun sets, position the mirror to reflect light into the water; also in the mirror will be the vision of your true love.

- **Look in the Lake Spell**—In Finland, a maiden is said to be able to spot her future mate at midnight on Midsummer Eve (Summer Solstice). Similar to the preceding spell, this one requires you to look into a lake to see the face of your love.

- **Star of Destiny Spell**—One Russian folk belief says that if an unmarried maiden sees a shooting star, wherever it lands will be the physical location of her future spouse.

- **Besom Blossom of Love Spell**—Most people associate magic and witches with brooms. In Celtic witchcraft, a ritual broom is called a besom and is used for both cleansing and prophecy. Folk magic says that if you sweep your bedroom while naked with a ritual broom on Yule or Midwinter's Night, you will dream of your future wife or husband. I must confess this spell sounds a little chilly for my comfort zone.

- **Hemp Seed Love Spell**—Another Celtic-based belief says that sowing a hemp seed on the morning of New Year's Day will bring a vision or dream of the future spouse. Recite an incantation in the manner of *"With this joyous seed I sow, may my love come and grow."*

- **Save Me**—This is less of a spell and more of a prophecy, but it is said that if you are drowning, in dreams or reality, the person who saves you will be your future husband or wife.

Foods for Romantic Love

Seduction is best begun at the table. An argument could be made that taste is your most erotic sense. It involves all the others: your mouth begins to water as you see food or another delicacy, then you smell it, you hear it going in ... being consumed, you feel it on your tongue, and finally you taste it. The recipes here are a delight for your table and your tongue.

Roasted Rose Chicken

One of my favorite films is *Like Water for Chocolate*, adapted from the novel by Laura Esquivel. In the film, the main character prepares an elegant meal of fowl with rose petal sauce. The petals impart a delicate taste and scent to the poultry, evoking sensuality on many different levels. This simple recipe can be roasted in the oven or cooked in a slow cooker. Prepare this whenever you want to grace your table with loving blessings.

INGREDIENTS:

2 tablespoons butter

1 tablespoon fresh rose petals

1 4-pound chicken

½ cup rose water

½ cup chicken broth

¼ teaspoon salt

¼ teaspoon white pepper

¼ teaspoon black pepper

>> Cream butter and add rose petals; mix thoroughly to combine. Wash and clean chicken and rub skin with rose butter. Sear meat in a frying pan until all sides are lightly golden. Remove from frying pan, place in a roaster pan, and cover with water, broth, salt, and pepper. Bake in 400-degree oven for 1½ hours, or place in slow cooker on low for 8–9 hours, adjusting time to be sure chicken is cooked through. When a meat thermometer is inserted in the thickest part of the chicken, it should reach 180 degrees. Remove from the oven (or slow cooker) and let sit for 15 minutes before serving. Share with your true loves and enjoy!

Chocolate-Dipped Strawberries Recipe for Love

Strawberries are one of the many plants ruled by Venus. My Scottish ancestors had a strawberry on their family crest, and suffice it to say, I have a deep and abiding love for this fruit. Like many aphrodisiac foods, even its very appearance is overtly sexual. This recipe combines two great romantic pleasures—both strawberries and chocolate—to conjure up some sweet romance.

INGREDIENTS:

1 pound strawberries, washed and dried

2 tablespoons butter

8 ounces bittersweet chocolate (chunks or chips)

≫ To make dipping easier, leave the leaves on your strawberries. Melt butter and chocolate in a double boiler. Dip strawberries one at a time into melted chocolate. Cool in the refrigerator for at least 15 minutes. Enjoy with your love.

Fizzy Borage Punch

Both the Greeks and Romans believed that the herb borage imparted one with supreme courage, vital for any love affair. Its tiny blue-purple flowers make a beautiful topper for this simple punch.

INGREDIENTS:

2 cups chilled red wine or grape juice

2 cups orange-flavored seltzer

¼ cup borage flowers

>> Combine wine (or juice) and seltzer. Chill mixture for an hour or longer. Top with borage flowers and serve.

Chapter Three

POTIONS FOR PASSIONS . . . AND SPELLS TOO

Passion, affection, affliction, lust, worship, devotion—it doesn't matter what name you call it, it drives men and madness the world around. In this chapter, you will discover spells to spark passion or rekindle it. In this particular magical area, please take extra care to protect yourself and ask only for exactly what you want. Use divination if at all possible to receive extra guidance and direction when opening up the floodgates of passion. The word *ecstasy* itself means transcendence. We could spend an entire lifetime studying the sensual delights of sex magic. This chapter is only a dip in the sacred waters of passionate sexuality, so please explore and enjoy.

Every culture around the globe has deities, rituals, and rites regarding passion.

The practice of Tantra is one of the most widely known forms of sexual magic. Ironically, its exact origins are disputed, but the practices today can be found within Hinduism, Buddhism, and Neo-Pagan (including New Age) practices.

Many theorize that in ancient times original Tantric practitioners used bodily fluids as sacred offerings to the deities. That theory has been contested; however, most are in agreement that traditional Hindu Tantric practices revolve around the postponement of orgasm in favor of higher states of enlightenment through this discipline. Under the guidance of a teacher, sexual, physical, and emotional energy would be raised and sustained for a series of days or weeks, bringing about a more intense connection to divinity.

Modern times have seen many embrace this ancient devotion to pleasure in their current spiritual practice. For those wishing to go down this route, I recommend learning more and seeking out some modern practitioners for guidance. Being a priestess or priest of sexual love is serious working that ultimately prepares us all for the future. Sacred sex can and does open the veil between worlds. As with most real magic, the presence of a teacher to help guide you in this process is invaluable. Please choose someone you trust and care for. I have, however, included a few Tantric-inspired spells in this chapter to help you get started raising your sacred sexual energy on your own. Sexual energy is a divine and powerful force we all possess.

There are a lot of shades to erotic magic—way more than fifty, probably more like five hundred. This chapter includes some kinky spells and some that border on the sexually coercive. Earlier I mentioned how people often use underwear or clothing as a binding element in their love magic. Many people take sex magic one step further and use menstrual blood or semen as a component of the spell. A common folk practice is even to mix these things into a person's food. I know of one questionable practitioner who tried to feed menstrual blood to her boyfriend in some hamburger when he quickly decided it wasn't for him. He fed it to the dog, and that dog was devoted to her till the day he died.

Candles: In Fiery Lust We Trust . . .

Maybe it's pride that makes me mention this again, or maybe cautious embarrassment, but if I'm honest about the first time I made love to my partner, we set the neighboring ancestor altar on fire. We didn't do it on purpose or anything like that; we were honestly too busy. All great love deserves a spark. We just didn't intend for it to happen exactly like that.

Tantric Treasure Meditation Candle

The goal of this candle is to amplify your natural sexual energy and connect it to the universal forces of sacred power. It is not about orgasm or release, but rather increase and purification. Here, you will choose both a yantra (or a sacred symbol) to focus your energy into and a mantra to say during the spell. These can be as simple or complex as you choose to make them.

INGREDIENTS:

1 red votive candle

candle holder

4 drops basil oil

4 drops jasmine oil

4 drops bergamot oil

chosen yantra

chosen mantra

>> Place the votive candle in the candle holder on your working altar. Place the basil, jasmine, and bergamot oil on the candle. Place your yantra, or symbol, in front of the candle and light it. Say your mantra one or multiple times to help attune and purify your energy. Continue until the candle has burned down completely. This is a helpful meditation spell to perform each month on the full moon as part of a larger regimen to improve your sexual energy.

Love Me Long Long Thyme Candle

This candle is crafted to bring about long-lasting love and passion. It can be used to rekindle or get the romance sweetly flowing in a relationship.

INGREDIENTS:

3 drops thyme oil

3 drops rose oil

3 drops ylang ylang oil

3 drops musk oil

1 red seven-day candle in glass

>> Place the thyme, rose, musk, and ylang ylang oils on the candle. Burn for seven nights, culminating on the full moon. Dispose of the remains at a cross-roads, if at all possible.

Very Violet Vixen Candle

The energy of this candle will help you tap into deep, unbridled passion and lust. Violet is the color of royalty, and it is also used for unusual pleasures.

INGREDIENTS:

glass candle holder

spring water

6 grains of paradise seeds

1 violet votive candle

6 drops violet oil

6 drops patchouli oil

3 drops neroli oil

>> Place the candle holder on your working altar. Pour a small amount of water in the bottom and then add the grains of paradise. Place the votive candle on top. Drip the oils on top of the votive and light. Inhale deeply as you feel your sensual energy rising.

Rings of Fire Candle

Use this candle whenever you are getting ready for a fiery night of love. It creates a radiant circle of passion that you can use as you wish.

INGREDIENTS:

6 drops patchouli oil

6 drops vanilla oil

6 drops ylang ylang oil

6 drops freesia oil

1 red seven-day pull-out candle

red glitter

≫ Pour oils out onto a flat plate. Roll candle in mixture and then cover with glitter. Place in candle holder and light whenever needed.

Sweet Seduction Candle

This candle spell will help gently set the stage for seduction. Use it to create an irresistible arena for passionate pleasures.

INGREDIENTS:

1 yellow votive candle
glass holder
3 drops ylang ylang oil
3 drops hibiscus oil

>> Place the candle in the holder. Put drops of oil on the candle and light just before you are about to start your seduction.

Mary Magdalene Enchantress Candle

Biblical legend has cast Mary Magdalene as a temptress and a fallen woman who found her way in the end. Many believe her story was in reality a much different one, a story of feminine power and sensual command. Try this candle spell to attract passion and beauty to you, and see for yourself the gifts of this ancient heroine.

INGREDIENTS:

picture of Mary Magdalene
6 drops lily oil
6 drops jasmine oil
6 drops myrrh oil

1 purple seven-day candle in glass
plate/bowl

>> Place oils on the candle. Take a picture of Mary
Magdalene and put the plate/bowl on top. Place the
candle on top of the plate/bowl. Light whenever you
wish to invoke the sacred power of this legendary
woman.

Starry Starry Night Passion Candle

Stars and planets have been an important part of
magic since the dawn of mankind. Even today, astrol-
ogy can be a useful tool in realizing your desires. As
far as love and passion are concerned, we can use the
astrological charts of our lovers and ourselves to help

amplify the sacred connection. This spell uses the symbols of the moon signs of you and your love to help improve this union. The moon is said to represent your emotions. You will need the exact birth time to determine this correctly. This spell is designed to bring two specific lovers together in passion.

INGREDIENTS:
moon sign astrological symbols for your partner and you
astrological symbol for Venus
red seven-day pull-out candle
6 drops ylang ylang oil
6 drops orange blossom oil
3 drops gardenia oil

≫ Carve the symbols on the candle; place your moon sign on the right, your lover's on the left, and the Venus symbol in the center. Cover the candle with the oils. Rub the oils in from the center upward, and then from the center downward. Place the candle back into the glass. Wash your hands. Light the candle on the eve of the full moon and every night afterward until it is finished. You may extinguish it each night for safety purposes, but be sure to say the words *"Even though I extinguish you, may your spiritual fire burn forever."*

Sex Magic Money Manifestation Candle Spell

Very often the type of sex magic people engage in is for manifestation. The premise is simple: two (or more) people will have sex and direct their energy toward a desired monetary result.

INGREDIENTS:

small piece parchment paper

glass candle holder

1 tablespoon tap water

1 red votive candle

3 drops rose oil

3 drops heliotrope oil

3 drops galangal oil

>> Write your financial desires on the parchment along with a symbol for wealth (a dollar sign or other symbol). Place the paper under the candle holder. Put the tap water in the bottom of the candle holder. Place the candle inside. Put the oils on top of the candle and light just before sex. During the sex act, remember to focus your energy at the candle, charging and blessing it. These types of spells can be very strong, so be prepared.

Magnetic Attraction Candle

In Hoodoo and other types of folk magic, lodestone is frequently used to attract things to you. As a natural magnet, it will help bring you your desires—in this case, some of the most lusty delights you can imagine.

INGREDIENTS:

glass candle holder

1 small piece lodestone

1 red votive candle

3 drops patchouli oil

3 drops Egyptian musk oil

3 drops jasmine oil

1 pinch iron filings

≫ Place the candle holder on your working altar. Place the lodestone and the candle into the holder. Put the patchouli, musk, and jasmine oil on the top of the candle and light. Say the following incantation or one of your own choosing: *"May love and passion be drawn to me, new heights of ecstasy and pleasure I'll see."* When the candle has burned down, you may dispose of it at the nearest crossroads.

Sacred Oils for Sensuality and Seduction

Using oils is one of the most practical ways of bringing passion into your life. In ancient times, Cleopatra and other legendary women were said to use oils to enhance their sexual power. Please do a small skin test before using the oils liberally because you never know what you can have a reaction to; as they say, "One man's pleasure can be another man's poison." However, after you have discovered your sensitivities, you can wear the other oils on your Heart chakra or your Root chakra, or on your pressure and pleasure points like your wrists and your neck. Or you can even place them on the soles of your feet so you will be divinely guided toward love and passion.

Aphrodite Oil

Aphrodite is one of the most popular goddesses of all time. She is in charge of all matters of beautiful love and inspired passion. Use this oil to bring love and passion on every level.

INGREDIENTS:
9 drops rose oil
9 drops sandalwood oil
3 drops cedarwood oil
1 small carnelian crystal
sweet almond oil for base

≫ Combine all ingredients together in a glass bottle or jar. Leave it on your windowsill for 24 hours where both the sun and moon rays will fall on it. Wear this oil daily for best results.

Lilith Oil

Referred to as an enchantress, hag, witch, demon, harlot, and murderer . . . , Lilith is the dark goddess of your dreams. Many believe that Lilith may be related to the early goddesses Inanna and Ishtar, but no matter what you call her or whom she stands next to, she is fierce. Lilith is one of the most ancient sensual goddesses in existence. She has become a cross-cultural voice of freedom and equality for women. This spell oil will let you explore your own night side and secret sensual desires. Wear this whenever you want to deeply connect with this goddess's energy.

INGREDIENTS:
3 drops patchouli oil
6 drops musk oil
3 drops cinnamon oil
½ ounce sweet almond oil
glass bottle

» Mix the oils together in a glass bottle. Rub the bottle between your hands to charge it.

Love Potion Number 9 Oil

Like the famous spell in the song of the same name, this formula is designed to quickly bring love to you, along with new insights and romantic opportunities.

INGREDIENTS:

3 drops bergamot oil

5 drops cinnamon oil

3 drops jasmine oil

3 drops magnolia oil

½ ounce sweet almond oil

glass bottle

>> Mix all ingredients together in a glass bottle. Rub the bottle between your hands to charge it with your energy. Wear on your person or add a few drops to a bath to bring love.

Love Potion Number 11 Oil

This oil is basically Love Potion Number 9—just turned up a few more notches. It is a strong and very effective formula.

INGREDIENTS:

3 drops bergamot oil

9 drops musk oil

3 drops patchouli oil

9 drops ylang ylang oil

½ ounce sweet almond oil

glass bottle

>> Mix all ingredients together in a glass bottle. Close tightly and place under your pillow. Sleep with the bottle for one night to charge it with your energy. Use this oil generously whenever lusty feelings are needed.

Powerful Passion Oil

Use this strongly sensual blend to bring about powerful passion in your romantic relationships.

INGREDIENTS:
3 drops cardamom oil
3 drops orange blossom oil
3 drops musk oil
3 drops patchouli oil
sweet almond oil for base
glass bottle

>> Combine all ingredients in a small glass bottle. Rub the bottle between your hands to charge it with your energy. Wear the oil before any and all intimate encounters.

Pomba Gira Turn Me On Oil

Pomba Gira is a very passionate deity from the Brazilian Umbanda pantheon. Frequently shown with bare breasts and a necklace of skulls, she is a patron of women of the night and a champion of all their sexual skills. One of the most amazing things about her is that she is unashamed and proud, a true feminine warrior. Use this oil to connect with Pomba Gira's sensual power energetically.

INGREDIENTS:
1 shot of whiskey
¼ ounce coconut oil
3 drops patchouli oil
3 drops amber oil

≫ Before starting the spell, pour out the shot of whiskey at a three-way crossroads, the place where three roads meet. Pomba Gira is said to be the owner of these special locales. Warm the coconut oil till it is liquid; then add the patchouli and amber oil. Rub the blend on your body to experience delirious spinning and complete passion. Use cautiously.

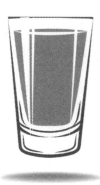

Wrap Myself Around You Massage Oil

This blend is great to share with your partner during your nights and days of erotic adventure. The sandalwood and rose will open up your hearts and minds and allow for a deeper connection on the physical plane.

INGREDIENTS:

10 drops sandalwood oil

10 drops rose oil

½ cup sweet almond oil

» Add the oils together. Use the blend to massage your partner, being careful at first on your gentle parts until you see how you react to the oils. Enjoy.

Spells and Recipes to Spice It Up

Rock this Bed Spell

Crystals and sacred geometry combine here in this magic spell to help you coax the heights of passion to your bed and keep them there. It is great to use when you're in a new relationship or when you get a new bed. Perform this spell on the full moon for the most effective results.

INGREDIENTS:

2 carnelian crystals

2 sunstone crystals

1 cup rose water

1 cup river water

1 large bowl

1 red votive candle

6 drops ylang ylang oil

3 drops tuberose oil

3 drops vanilla oil

>> Place the waters and the crystals in the bowl. Place the candle in the center of the bowl. Put the ylang ylang, tuberose, and vanilla oils on top of the candle and light it. You may say the following invocation or create one of your own choosing: *"Infuse these stones with this sensual brew, sacred oils and waters in a sexual stew. May extraordinary passions now come to me, when I wish in the day, or in the night, So mote it be!"* When the candle has burned out, remove the crystals from the water and place near the four legs or posts of your bed. Leave them there as long as you wish the magic to continue. You can dispose of the remaining water and candle outside on the earth.

Hot Pants Ginger Spell

This simple and effective spell will invigorate your nether regions. Use it in the hours leading up to a hot date or encounter to help you get ready for passion.

INGREDIENTS:
5 drops sesame oil
1 small piece ginger root
piece of red natural fabric

>> Place oil on the ginger root, wrap tightly in fabric, and place in your pocket.

Stick It to Me Cinnamon Gris-Gris Spell

Cinnamon sticks, red ribbons, and lusty oils all combine in this gris-gris spell to grant you powerful passion and sexual energy. Use this spell to invigorate your relationship.

INGREDIENTS:
2 small cinnamon sticks
2 drops patchouli oil
2 drops musk oil

2 drops vervain oil
2 strawberry leaves
2 red ribbons

≫ Write your name on each of the cinnamon sticks; then write your partner's name over yours. On each stick, place 1 drop each of patchouli oil, musk oil, and vervain oil. Place the sticks next to each and wrap in strawberry leaves. Tie the whole thing together at the top with one of the red ribbons, using three knots. Then do the same thing at the bottom with the ribbon, again using three knots. Carry the sticks in your pocket until you have the lusty encounter you desire. This working is best done on the full moon.

Falling in Love Again Gris-Gris Spell

The moment Marlene Dietrich walked on to the silver screen, she made history. This sensual iconoclast defined sexuality in a whole new way. This herbal gris-gris mix should be put under the bed or sprinkled around the bedroom to increase lusty passions on your own terms. You can use it to increase your attractiveness and sexual confidence in any situation.

INGREDIENTS:

¼ cup dried sweet woodruff

¼ cup dried rose petals

¼ cup edelweiss flowers

large bowl

>> Combine all ingredients in a large bowl. Mix together well with your hands. Place in a small cloth bag under your bed or sprinkle about your home to bring passion.

BDSM Spell

The world is a different place these days; even bondage has gone mainstream. Housewives are shopping for rope at the hardware store, and people are exploring their sexual limits. I remember doing a pagan event not so many years ago where another presenter was teaching a pagan BDSM workshop. We all chuckled as one of the first questions was from someone who thought *BDSM* was short for Buddhism. In this spell you will be casting a sacred circle for all your toys, tools, and play so you may have a heightened experience. You can either cast the space before a session or just use it to bless your tools. The choice is yours.

INGREDIENTS:
white or black sheet
1 black votive candle
glass candle holder
½ cup peppermint
½ cup rose petals
¼ cup frankincense tears
3 drops ylang ylang oil
pinch of black pepper
bowl

>> Lay the sheet out on the floor. Place the candle in the candle holder in the center and light. Combine the peppermint, rose petals, frankincense, ylang ylang oil, and peppermint in the bowl and combine well. Sprinkle the mixture out on the sheet in a large circle moving clockwise. If you wish, you may now place your toys or tools in the circle to bless while the candle burns. Once the candle has burned down, gather up the sheet by the four corners and shake it out onto the earth.

Foods for Passion

Magical seductions are performed every day by people who are unaware of what they are really doing. The list of things we can use as edible potions for passion right in our kitchen ranges from apricots to yarrow wine.

Vanilla Apricot Granola Recipe

Vanilla is a sensual delicacy that comes from the beautiful orchid flower. It has been a sacred food for thousands of years. In Central America, it is the stuff of legend. Originally, it was used as an incense to perfume the sacred temples. Vanilla is said to increase blood flow and, thereby, passionate encounters. Make and eat this recipe whenever you need to get things flowing in the right direction.

INGREDIENTS:

4 cups rolled oats

½ cup chopped walnuts

½ cup chopped pecans

1 cup raw sunflower seeds

½ cup unsalted butter or margarine

½ cup honey

2 teaspoons vanilla extract

¼ teaspoon ground nutmeg

½ teaspoon ground cinnamon

½ cup diced dried apricots

¼ cup golden raisins, or sultanas

>> In a large bowl, combine the oats, nuts, and sunflower seeds. Melt the butter and honey over a low flame. Remove from heat and add vanilla, nutmeg, and cinnamon, stirring well. Pour over oat mixture and stir until coated. Pour mixture out onto two large baking sheets, and place in a 350-degree oven for 35–45 minutes, stirring frequently. Cool and add apricots and golden raisins. This recipe makes 8–9 servings.

Oshun Seduction Salsa Recipe

Food is one of the simplest spells we can perform. Frequently, I have psychic clients for spellwork who don't know how to effect change in their lives. A recipe is an easy way to do this for yourself or others. The next time you have the opportunity to feed the one you love, consider making this seductive delicacy to connect to Oshun, the African Orisha of love.

INGREDIENTS:

½ cup mango, diced
½ cup peaches, diced
2 cups plum tomatoes, seeded and diced
½ cup chopped Vidalia onion
1 clove garlic, minced
1 teaspoon chili powder
1 teaspoon smoked paprika
1 tablespoon white wine vinegar
hot sauce to taste
salt and pepper

>> Mix all the ingredients together in a large bowl. Stir counterclockwise as you invoke the positive energy of love into the mixture. Chill in the refrigerator one hour or longer. Serve with corn chips. Enjoy with those you love.

Marinated Olives

The olive tree symbolizes peace and abundance. It is one of the oldest culti-vated trees in recorded history. The poet Homer called olive oil "liquid gold." This is a fairly easy make-ahead recipe that will keep for at least a week in the refrigerator. You can top it off with extra olive oil if necessary. This recipe will open up your opportunities for passionate love with your partner.

INGREDIENTS:

1 cup black olives, pitted

½ cup green pimento-stuffed olives

3 tablespoons champagne vinegar

1 large bay leaf

1 tablespoon crushed rosemary

3 sprigs thyme, removed from stalks

½ teaspoon oregano

1 teaspoon fresh basil, minced

1 teaspoon fresh parsley, minced

2 tablespoons capers

¼ cup olive oil

>> Combine all ingredients and let stand refrigerated for one hour up to one week. It is very sensual and should, if at all possible, be hand fed to your lover.

Fig Fantasy Appetizers

Figs were reported to be Cleopatra's favorite food, and it is easy to see why this beloved fruit has been cherished for centuries. Like many of the aphrodisiac foods, part of its power comes from its resemblance to female genitalia. These delicious treats are quick and easy to prepare, yet look and taste elegant and sophisticated. This amazing recipe will bring passionate feelings from tongue to toes.

INGREDIENTS:

2 tablespoons cream cheese

1 tablespoon wildflower honey

1 tablespoon walnuts, chopped

1 tablespoon candied ginger, chopped

10 slices lightly toasted French bread

1 fresh fig, sliced thin

>> Mix cheese, honey, ginger, and walnuts together in a small bowl. Spread a thin layer of the mixture on each bread slice and top with a few slices of fig. Serve immediately. This recipe serves 10 as an appetizer, or 2–3 along with a salad as a tasty entrée. Makes a great sensual invitation to romance.

Yarrow Wine Punch

In ancient times, the Celts made a mead (honey wine) with yarrow. You can make your own yarrow and honey treat blessed by the moon by following the recipe here. It will help you find direction and luck in sensual pursuits.

INGREDIENTS:

1 gallon white wine
½ cup yarrow blossoms
½ cup lemon balm leaves
¼ cup honey
1 quart strawberries, washed and halved
1 quart blueberries, washed
1 bottle champagne

>> Combine wine and herbs in a large crock and let sit out overnight. The next day add honey, berries, and champagne and chill for 6 hours or longer. Serve chilled.

Simply Sensual Flower Fudge

This easy recipe will bring sensual pleasure into your life. It uses two common flowers—red roses and lavender—to help improve your sensual awareness and joy of sex.

INGREDIENTS:

2 cups semi-sweet chocolate chips
2 tablespoons lavender blossoms, dried and ground fine
1 tablespoon red rose petals, dried and ground fine
1 can sweetened condensed milk
3 tablespoons butter

>> Place chocolate, lavender, roses, and condensed milk into a double boiler and heat until the chocolate is melted. Stir frequently. Add butter and mix to combine. Pour into a 9-inch × 9-inch square pan that has been lined with wax paper. Chill until firm. Enjoy with your lover to bring about sensual delights.

Chapter Four

SPELLS FOR MARRIAGE AND SACRED UNIONS

"We are sun and moon, dear friend; we are sea and land. It is not our purpose to become each other; it is to recognize each other, to learn to see the other and honor him for what he is: each the other's opposite and complement."

—HERMANN HESSE, Narcissus and Goldmund

There comes a time when love progresses to the next level, and marriage and commitment can come into view. Some of these workings are designed to incorporate into a wedding or handfasting ceremony you are planning, and some are for making the conditions favorable for a desired marriage proposal. There is even one to help you and your partner find and move into your ideal home.

When we talk about marriage and handfasting, one important component is most certainly the vows. The vows are a spell in and of themselves, a spell performed by two or more people with the help of friends, family, and clergy if they so choose. There are two different kinds of vows: those that are spoken and those that are repeated. Magically, I prefer repeated vows, as repetition is one of the cornerstones of spell-crafting and ritual. Customarily, words are repeated three times to ensure their transmissions to the God, Goddess, and the universe. You can choose to write your vows yourselves or with the aid of your spiritual teachers and mentors. Be sure to highlight, salute, reinforce, and honor the deep love and passion you share, and the sacred commitment you are about to make. You can do this with words that are spoken, but you can also do this in other ways.

Recently, I performed a commitment ceremony for my partner and me, and I took many of the quotes I wished to share in my vows of love to him and made them into artistic creations. I wrote the words on candle holders, vases, and goblets, and used them to visually illustrate what I needed to express. This would make a lovely idea for a larger ceremony as well. In addition to the words, you can also use the oils, incense, candles, gris-gris, and other magics here to show and support the love between your and your spouse or spouses.

Herbal Spells and Incense for Marriage

Tradition says marriage is for sprinkling, and now-adays most modern lovers have given up throwing rice for the more bird-friendly alternative of rose petals or glitter. This section shows you some spells to use both at the altar and to help you get there happily.

Going to the Chapel or Temple Herbal Mix

One easy thing you can do to help magically prepare your sacred space before your wedding or handfast-ing ceremony is to make an herbal mix for sprinkling around. You can spread this around the morning of the wedding or the day before the ceremony. It is effective used either indoors or outdoors. You could even add it to the walkway for the flower girl to spread around. This will bring blessings of deep love and success to your union.

INGREDIENTS:

1 cup rose petals, dried

½ cup thyme, dried

3 drops orchid oil

3 drops vanilla oil

>> Place rose petals and thyme together in a large bowl. Add the orchid oil and vanilla oil. Mix together with your hands till combined. Sprinkle liberally.

Marriage Mojo Bag

Gris-gris bags, also known as mojo bags, are magical medicine bags that have been used for centuries in New Orleans Voodoo and Hoodoo traditions. The following is used to strengthen and improve the already-existing bond between a long-term couple. It is designed to combine your energies together and take you to the next level of interconnectedness. Red and pink rose petals are included to attract love and romance. Honeysuckle represents togetherness, as even the flowers themselves intertwine on the vine. Gardenia is a flower used to bring joyous love, while garnet is traditionally exchanged as part of a marital pledge and was once used for engagement rings.

INGREDIENTS:
½ cup red and pink rose petals
¼ cup honeysuckle blossoms
¼ cup gardenia blossoms
pinch garnet dust or garnet gemstone
red gris-gris bag

>> Combine all ingredients on the eve of the full moon. Fill the red gris-gris bag with as much of the herbal blend as possible. Remove contents of bag and refill every Friday until you have used up all of the mixture. This spell works best when both partners wear a bag.

Immortal Beloved Vampire Incense

People have an obsession with vampires, born of legend and shrouded in white darkness and mystery. It is easy to see their appeal. This incense spell will help foster a deep and passionate bond between lovers that will survive the ages, the kind that seems to come with vampires just as often as fangs.

INGREDIENTS:

1 tablespoon copal resin
1 tablespoon myrrh resin
3 drops dove's blood oil
3 drops dragon's blood oil
self-lighting charcoal

>> Combine all ingredients together in a small bowl on the eve of the full moon. Leave the bowl outside overnight where it will be moonstruck by the rays of the evening. Bring it back in your home, throw it gently into the air, and catch it. The purpose is to bless it with the energy of the invisibles. Burn the incense on self-lighting charcoal whenever you wish to cement and strengthen the bond between you and your life, or afterlife, partner.

Blissful Oils to Bring on Wedded Bliss

Here you will find magical oils for marriage. Oils are both sensual and subtle, making them just right for using in your marriage workings.

Marry Me Oil

When you wish someone will get down on bended knee, use this spell, which contains ingredients to bring about favorable conditions for the sweetest of proposals to happen. Remember to keep an open mind and an open heart, and your love's pledge will come to you.

INGREDIENTS:

6 drops frangipani oil

3 drops gardenia oil

6 drops honeysuckle oil

½ ounce sweet almond oil

glass bottle

>> Combine all ingredients in a glass bottle. Shake well to combine.

Same Soul Oil

If we are lucky in love, our bodies and our souls combine with another. Emily Brontë wrote, "Whatever our souls are made of, his and mine are the same." This oil salutes the union of two souls joined blissfully as one. It will help provide deep love, emotional connections, and fidelity.

INGREDIENTS:

12 drops myrtle oil

6 drops tuberose oil

6 drops sandalwood oil

glass bottle

>> Combine all ingredients in a glass bottle on the full moon. To charge the mixture, pass it back and forth between you and your love three times. Wear as needed to deepen your bond whether you are together or apart.

Damballa and Aida Wedo Marriage Oil

Damballa and his wife, Aida Wedo, the divine serpents of Haitian Vodou, are the creators of the universe. They form the serpent and the rainbow of legend that intertwine to bring sacred blessings to all. Use this oil to strengthen the long-term connection between you and your partner. It will also help you support and encourage each other.

INGREDIENTS:

6 drops galangal oil

6 drops myrrh oil

¼ ounce sweet almond oil

glass bottle

1 small piece snakeskin

>> Add the myrrh and galangal to the sweet almond oil in a glass bottle. Place the snakeskin inside the

bottle. Rub the bottle between your hands to charge it with positive energy.

Truly Madly Deeply Blissfully Oil

This oil is inspired by one of my favorite films, *Truly Madly Deeply*. In it, the lovers challenge themselves to list all the ways in which they love each other. Charge this spell with the back-and-forth words of two lovers. This oil will help solidify your connection and further you on your journey together.

INGREDIENTS:
5 drops ylang ylang oil
5 drops magnolia oil
5 drops jasmine oil
¼ ounce sweet almond oil
glass bottle

>> Mix the oils together in a glass bottle. Throw the bottle gently into the air to give it the blessing of the spirit world. Next, exchange words with your love to charge the spell. This will go as follows:

" I love you truly . . ."
" I love you truly, madly, . . ."
"I love you truly, madly, deeply, . . ."
"I love you truly, madly, deeply, blissfully, . . ."

• You can go on as long as you like. After you charge this spell, feel free to use it whenever you need to feel the bond between you and your love, when you are apart, on your anniversary, whenever feels necessary.

White Wedding Oil

Featuring fragrant white botanicals, this blessing oil is designed specifically for your special day. You can wear this oil or place a drop into centerpiece candles to spread joyous love throughout the entire celebration.

INGREDIENTS:

3 drops apple blossom oil

3 drops jasmine oil

3 drops gardenia oil

3 drops honeysuckle oil

¼ ounce sweet almond oil for base

glass bottle

≫ Combine all ingredients together in a glass bottle on the full moon. If you like, you may say the following incantation or use one of your own: *"By the sacred power of these flowers four, Speed love and blessings to our door."*

Come Together Oil

This oil blend will bring you and your lover together on all levels. It includes magical elements for heat, romance, and sacred union. Use it when you want to come together.

INGREDIENTS:
3 drops cinnamon oil
3 drops tuberose oil
3 drops violet oil
sweet almond oil for base
glass bottle

≫ Combine all oils together in a small glass bottle. Sleep with the bottle under your pillow or mattress for one night to charge it. Wear the oil whenever you and your partner are seeking a deeper and more united connection.

Butterfly Transformation Wedding Oil

One of the most amazing weddings I have ever attended was a destination event in Jamaica where two of my godkids got married. The sun, the sea, the sand, and their amazing love were truly an inspiration. On the plane home, however, I sat next to a bridesmaid and heard about a wedding that was not so nice. This woman had just come from a very expensive affair that had mishap after mishap, including an amazing gesture in which hundreds of butterflies were to be released as part of the ceremony to symbolize the couple's love. Nature had another idea. The problem was that when the couple opened the box, all

they could say was, "Dem dead butterflies." Needless to say, that was only the tip of the iceberg, and that wedding didn't go off. This butterfly oil will help you make the marvelous change from your old life to the next—no dead butterflies here!

INGREDIENTS:

6 drops heliotrope oil

6 drops jasmine oil

6 drops carnation oil

6 drops hibiscus oil

¼ ounce sweet almond oil

glass bottle

>> Place all ingredients together into a glass bottle. Throw the bottle up into the air gently three times to charge it with the energy of the air. Wear the oil on your wedding day or place in simmering pots around the room at your wedding reception to joyously bless the event.

Sun-kissed Massage Oil

Every culture has its own special customs for marriage and sacred unions. In the Hindu tradition, calendula flowers are often used as part of the ceremony. They are placed on walls, floors, and participants to bless the event. This massage oil spell uses those sacred flowers, and others florals that salute the Sun, to bring you blessed delights in your marriage.

INGREDIENTS:

5 drops calendula oil
5 drops sunflower (*Helianthus*) oil
5 drops rose oil
5 drops vanilla oil
sweet almond oil for base
glass bottle

≫ Combine all ingredients in a glass bottle on the full
moon. Leave outside for one full day or on a windowsill where the sun's rays will bless and charge it with
its energy. My advice would be to test it before your
wedding night, but once you are positive neither of
you have a difficult skin reaction, you can use this
sun-kissed oil as often as the mood strikes you.

Candle Spells for Marriage

Many of the spells in this book use candles as a sacred flame to bring about the desired changes and success in your life. This section shows you many different ways to spiritually light the pathway to marriage.

Wedding Bells Candle Spell

Light this easy candle spell to increase your chances of a marriage proposal from your partner. It will allow you to focus your energy and that of the universe on bringing about your desires.

INGREDIENTS:
3 pink votive candles
glass candle holder
rose water
3 pinches orris root powder
9 drops jasmine oil
9 drops lavender oil

>> Place candle in glass holder with a small amount of rose water and a pinch of orris root in the bottom. Place 3 drops of jasmine and lavender oil on the top of the candle. Light the candle and envision your lover saying the words you wish to hear. Burn one candle each night for three nights leading up to the full moon.

Adam and Eve, or Adam and Steve, or Lesbians Candle Spell

There are many pre-made candles for love that you can purchase. This particular spell uses one of these candles designed to honor the biblical lovers Adam and Eve. Obviously, as the title says, you can substitute whatever relationship situation you are working with. Light this spell on the full moon if possible, to bring a deeper understanding and balance between a married or committed couple.

INGREDIENTS:
2 drops patchouli oil
2 drops apple blossom oil
1 juniper berry
1 pinch allspice
Adam and Eve candle in glass

>> Place the oils and spices on top of the candle and light in the bedroom of the couple. This will help foster love, ecstatic passion, and understanding between them.

Wedded Bliss Eve Candle

Light this candle the night before your wedding. It will help you gain clarity, focus, and hopefully some much-needed rest before the big day.

INGREDIENTS:

1 pink votive candle
glass candle holder
spring water
4 drops lavender oil
4 drops myrrh oil
4 drops sesame oil

>> Place the pink candle into the holder. Put a small amount of spring water in the bottom. Top with the oils and light. Inhale deeply as the candle burns, and focus on the joyous journey that lies ahead.

Juno Candle

Full of energy and joy, Juno is the Roman goddess of marriage and birth. Even the month of June is named for her. Because she is a moon goddess, this spell is most effective when performed on the full moon. It will bring guidance from the ancestors and blessings to your ceremony.

INGREDIENTS:

1 yellow votive candle

glass candle holder

3 drops bergamot oil

3 drops apple blossom oil

≫ Put the candle in the holder onto your working altar. Place oils on top of the candle. Light on the full moon nearest your wedding day to connect with the loving energy of this time-honored goddess.

Frigga Wedding Candle Spell

In the Norse pantheon, the goddess Frigga rules over marriage, the household, and the entire community. This would be a great candle to use as part of the altar on your wedding day, especially if you are incorporating elements of the Norse tradition on your big day.

INGREDIENTS:

candle holder

spring water

1 pinch lady's mantle herb, dried

1 white votive candle

1 key

3 drops birch oil

3 drops thyme oil

≫ Place the candle holder on your altar and pour some spring water in the bottom. Put a pinch of lady's mantle in the candle holder and then place the candle in the holder. Put the key in front of the candle on the altar. Put the birch and thyme oil on top of the candle and light it saying the following prayer or one of your own choosing:

"Blessed Goddess of the Hearth,
Bless our Sacred Fire, Our Union and this Place . . .
We Share with you these offerings
And give honor to your divine grace!"

Tie the Knot Spells

Traditional pagan handfasting ceremonies usually include a joining together of hands tied together with a cord or cords in a figure eight, a symbol of infinity. This is where the phrase "tie the knot" originally comes from. The length of the cords should be the same as the height of the individuals getting hand-fasted; some choose to use one cord, whereas others use three or more braided together. The couple can face each other, bind their right hands, or bind both hands together—the choice is yours. The decision of what colors to use is also usually determined by the couple themselves and generally follows these correspondences:

Red—Passion

Pink—Romantic love

Yellow—Devotion

Orange—Kindness and attraction

White—Pure love

Green—Success and growth

Blue—Truth

Purple—Spiritual and psychic connections

Gold—Energy and longevity

Among traditional Celtic handfastings, the period of union was meant to last a year and a day in order to give the couple a chance to sample the pairing. Nowadays many pagans use a handfasting in place of a more traditional wedding ceremony. As with the custom of jumping the broom, many non-pagans have even incorporated this element into their wedding rites, and as long as it is done respectfully, I am in full support. You may choose to begin or end your ceremony with the binding of your hands. Originally, you and your beloved would have remained tied together until you consummated your union, but nowadays life dictates you may need to disengage sooner. In that case, try to remove the cords as carefully as possible and save them to put with your wedding flowers and other sacred mementos of the day.

Wedding Dream Pillow Spell

This spell allows you to gain clear visions of your future spouse and married life. Record whatever you may remember in a dream journal upon waking. It may also help to do automatic writing or divination after this spell to gain further clarity and direction. If marriage is what you truly desire, this spell will help you find your way to the altar.

INGREDIENTS:

1 cup dried rose petals
1 tablespoon dried wormwood
1 tablespoon dried mugwort
1 tablespoon dried orange peel
enough pink natural fabric to make a pillow

>> Combine all the herbs together in a large bowl. Stir counterclockwise until all the ingredients are mixed

together. Use this mixture as a filling for a pillow made using the pink fabric. You can sew the pillow into a heart, circle, or square shape. If possible, keep the pillow on your bed until your vision and path to manifest it have become clear.

Unakite Togetherness Spell

The word *unakite* is derived from the Greek words meaning grow together. This is a stone of marriage, of deep and abiding partnerships. It would be a great addition to any handfasting or commitment ceremony.

INGREDIENTS:

2 pieces unakite (or 2 pieces unakite jewelry)
4 drops rose oil
1 cup river water
small bowl

>> Place all ingredients into the bowl. Leave the bowl outside on the night of the full moon to charge. The next morning remove the unakite and pour out the rest

of the contents under a large tree. The jewelry should be worn, or the crystals should be carried, by both partners from then on to ensure their bond.

Carnelian Courage Spell

Even though you truly love your partner, sometimes mustering up enough courage on your wedding day can become difficult. I had one friend whose parents made the couple have a civil ceremony before the expensive one for friends and family. The parents didn't trust them to go through with the ceremony on the big day, and they were right. . . . Though the two were married before a judge the week before, when the time came to say their vows in a ceremony that cost almost $100,000, they couldn't do it. Needless to say, their decision didn't go over well. Just like love, courage can be courted, and this spell will help you gain the necessary fortitude to step up to the altar and make the leap into your new life. Craft this working on the full moon before your wedding day.

INGREDIENTS:

1 yellow votive candle
glass candle holder
tap water
2 pieces carnelian crystal
3 drops frankincense oil
3 drops sweet pea oil
3 drops cedarwood oil

>> Place the candle in the holder (with a small amount of tap water in the bottom) on your working or wedding altar. Place the two carnelian crystals in front of it. Place one drop each of frankincense, sweet pea, and cedarwood oil on each crystal and on the candle. Light the candle. You and you partner together should say the follow words or ones of your own choosing:

> *"Grant me courage*
> *May my feet hold strong*
> *I love and cherish this person*
> *All the days and nights long."*

>> Breathe deeply and concentrate on the candle and on your partner as the candle burns down. When the candle is finished, take the crystals and carry them with you until your wedding day. After the ceremony, you can place them under your bed or on your home altar.

Lovers' Night Tarot Spell

In the language of the tarot, the Lovers card represents exactly what its name says and so much more. It is a partnership, a sacred complement, a half to help you realize a divine whole. You may use the Lovers card from your own tarot deck or choose one that inspires you from art or history. There are decks inspired or created by artists like Salvador Dali and Gustav Klimt, and even ones based on zombies and butterflies . . . choose wisely. Depending on which iconography you choose, you can use this spell to bring about a loving partnership in many ways: it can bring marriage, an intense sexual connection, or a choice to make a deeper commitment. Try to keep your focus and intent as clear as possible.

INGREDIENTS:
Lovers tarot card (from any deck, depending on your specific desires)
glass jar with lid
1 tea light
3 drops sweet orange oil
3 drops rose oil
3 drops lemon oil
2 drops sandalwood oil
1 cup spring water
1 cup May rainwater

>> Place the tarot card on your working altar. Put the glass jar on top and fill with oils and waters. Cover with the lid. Place the tea light on top of the jar and light. When the tea light extinguishes, place the Lovers card back in the deck, and the formula is ready to use. This mixture can be used as a floor wash for your wedding ceremony area or your honeymoon bedroom (and if you are too busy honeymooning, you can just put it under the bed before the fun starts).

Wedding Broom Spell

Weddings have always been an important time for rituals and traditions. One tradition says that a new bride needs something old, something new, something borrowed, and . . . a broom. The custom of "jumping the broom" has been around for hundreds of years. It has become a special blessing that the couple takes as they make their leap into a new journey together. In many ways, it is a symbol and a legacy that people continue today.

Over time, "jumping the broom" has been associated with African-American weddings because this was the closest thing to a wedding they, as slaves, were allowed. Slaves were cruelly denied access to traditional ceremonies and so much more. Some people consider the ritual to be an honoring and remembrance of the ancestors, while others choose to omit it because it is too painful a reminder of the basic privileges denied an oppressed people. The custom is not really an African-derived one at all. It gained popularity during slavery in the United States and has been revived in the past few decades. Re-creating meaning and tradition when so much has been lost over the years is a difficult business. The ritual broom, or besom, is actually more of a Celtic custom, but you still may choose to use it in your ceremony.

Some brooms include cowrie shells for prosperity, sunflowers for joy, roses or orchids for sweet love, or other magical elements. If at all possible, try to take the time and effort to craft your own broom. This particular broom spell will bring you both love and passion on your wedding day and throughout your relationship.

INGREDIENTS:

5 drops sunflower oil

5 drops orange blossom oil

1 small broom (or make your own by tying stalks to a stick and fastening with hemp cord)

5 red ribbons

5 pink ribbons

2 rose quartz crystals

>> Place the oils on the broom handle or stalk. Next, tie the ribbons one at at time, alternating between the red and the pink, to the bottom sweeping bristles of the broom. Glue the crystals to the broom handle. Leave the broom on a windowsill or outside overnight during the full moon so the moon's rays will bless it. Now it is ready to use as a blessing broom for your ceremony, or for jumping if you so choose.

St. Christopher Honeymoon Traveling Spell

A honeymoon is a joyous completion of a wedding ceremony. It is a blissful start to the new life you and your partner will have together. Many couples are lucky enough to travel to exotic locales for their ultimate romantic getaway. St. Christopher, the patron saint of travelers, lends his power to this spell to get you safely and successfully on your journey.

INGREDIENTS:

1 red votive candle

Psalm 17 (see Appendix A)

1 small picture of St. Christopher or St. Christopher medal

small bowl

3 drops frankincense oil

Florida water

3 stalks royal fern, often associated with St. Christopher

1 stalk comfrey

>> Place the red candle on your working altar and light it. Read Psalm 17 aloud. Place the St. Christopher picture under the bowl, or the medal inside the bowl, and add the oil and Florida water. Use the fern and comfrey stalks to brush your feet and those of your love to ensure safety for your future travels. Dispose of the stalks and the liquid under a large tree. Place the picture, or medal, in your luggage and have a wonderful trip!

Selenite Happy Home Spell

This spell is for committed couples or partners looking to find a home, or to improve the conditions of the home they already share. Use it before meeting with your real estate professional, mortgage broker, or anyone related to the home-buying process. This spell is best performed on the full moon.

INGREDIENTS:

glass candle holder

small piece selenite crystal

holy water

1 white votive candle

3 drops St. Joseph oil

≫ Place the candle holder and the crystal in the center of your working altar. Sprinkle a small amount of holy water in the bottom of the candle holder. Add the votive candle and put the drops of St. Joseph's oil on top. Light the candle and meditate on the vision of your ideal home while the candle burns. When it is finished, dispose of the candle wax in the trash. Be sure to remember to carry the crystal with you at all times until the home you desire and the means to get it manifest. Selenite is ruled by the moon and gets extra potency from being "moonstruck," so leave the crystal out overnight on the subsequent full moons whenever you need to recharge it.

Marriage Moon Bath

Take this bath together with your beloved on the eve before the full moon closest to your wedding. It will help you connect your emotions and bodies together, and bless your upcoming ceremony.

INGREDIENTS:

5 drops jasmine oil

5 drops rose oil

5 drops ylang ylang oil

5 drops orange blossom, or neroli oil

5 drops bergamot oil

1 cup May rainwater

1 cup rose water

1 handful fresh red rose petals

>> Combine all ingredients together in a warm bath. Bathe slowly with your partner, concentrating on the joyous path that lies ahead and the deep love you share. Feel free to repeat this spell each year on the full moon closest to your anniversary to strengthen your bond.

Marriage Foods

Wedding reception menus would do well to include recipes so everyone can share in the joy of the union. These recipes can also just be prepared for your love as part of the spells designed to open the way for marriage. Do your best to keep your mind positive and focused too when you are preparing these dishes; use an oil or candle to help, if you so choose.

Drunken Oshun Oranges

One traditional offering for Oshun, the Lucumi Orisha of love, is five oranges, given to ensure a successful marriage. Use this magical recipe to help open the door to her divine blessings and salute her energy as part of your wedding feast.

INGREDIENTS:

zest from 1 orange
zest from 1 lemon
1 cup water
½ cup sugar
5 tablespoons orange liqueur, like Grand Marnier
5 large oranges, peeled and sliced into rings crosswise

>> Take the zest from 1 orange and 1 lemon, and place in a saucepan with the cup of water. Cook for 5 minutes over medium heat. Remove zest from water by straining, and discard. Add sugar to liquid and boil for 5 minutes or until it begins to get syrupy. Remove from heat, add liqueur, and add to a slow cooker along with the orange rings. Cook on low heat for 2 hours until done. Serve chilled with fresh whipped cream. Makes 4–6 servings.

Wedding Roasted Asparagus

Asparagus is used as a traditional wedding dish in Scotland. It is eaten by the bride, groom, and the whole reception party and is thought to provide fertility, bounty, and ancestral blessings for the new union. (*Note:* Asparagus is known to turn your urine green, just so you don't think anything is amiss.)

INGREDIENTS:

2 pounds asparagus spears, trimmed

3 tablespoons olive oil

1 tablespoon lemon juice

1 tablespoon garlic, minced finely

salt and pepper to taste

>> Preheat oven to 350 degrees. Combine all ingredients in a large roasting pan and roast for 25–35 minutes. Check toward the end of cooking and be sure to remove the spears while they are tender but not overdone. Serves 6–8 people, but you can multiply for your own wedding reception.

Rose Rice Pudding (or Kheer)

This traditional South Asian dessert is most often prepared for celebratory religious feasts and weddings. It features rice for fertility, cardamom and roses for love, and coconut for purity and protection. You can use this spell to bring any or all of these elements to your celebration.

INGREDIENTS:

2 cups lowfat milk

1 cup coconut milk

1 tablespoon sugar

1 cup basmati rice

¼ cup golden raisins or sultanas

¼ teaspoon ground cardamom

1 teaspoon rose water
¼ cup chopped cashews
¼ cup chopped pistachios

>> Bring milk, coconut milk, and sugar up to a low simmer in a saucepan. Add rice, cover pan, and continue to simmer for approximately 20 minutes or until rice is tender. Stir in sultanas, cardamom, and rose water and cook for 1 minute longer. Spoon the mixture into serving bowls and top with nuts. Serves 4–5 people.

Classic Strawberry Shortcake with Cinnamon Whipped Cream

Strawberries are a member of the rose family, and these heart-shaped red beauties are a wonderful addition to your wedding-night menu. In France, strawberry soup is a traditional dish for newlyweds. Nutritionally, strawberries are high in vitamin C, folic acid, and zinc, as well as antioxidants. This recipe will help bring delicious love to all who eat it on the special day.

INGREDIENTS:
10 large strawberries, cored and sliced
1 tablespoon sugar
1 cup biscuit baking mix
⅓ cup milk
½ cup heavy cream
¼ teaspoon ground cinnamon

≫ Place strawberries in a non-metal bowl and toss with 1 tablespoon of the sugar. Set strawberry mixture aside. Mix together baking mix and milk; then drop batter by tablespoonfuls onto a greased cookie sheet. Bake at 400 degrees for 5–7 minutes or until golden brown. In a separate bowl, whip heavy cream together with sugar until stiff and then whisk in cinnamon. Slice biscuits in half, top with strawberry mix, cover with biscuit top, more strawberries, and top it all off with a dollop of whipped cream. Serves 2–3 people.

Chapter Five

FERTILITY SPELLS

Fertility can take many forms. At its core, it is about abundance, increase, and bounty. The medical profession has turned infertility into a billion-dollar business. I understand, because when trying to create life, it is sometimes neither cheap nor easy. Please be sure to also check with divination or other methods to determine the underlying causes of the infertility. It may be medical, and/or it may be psychological, in addition to spiritual, and all of those areas will need to be dealt with for the blessing of conception to happen.

I had a tarot client once who came to me for a consultation about her fertility. She had tried many times to conceive. The reading said she needed to obtain graveyard dirt for her ancestors and her husband's. She quickly started to argue. A spiritual prescription is just like a medical one: if you don't follow the advice, then the situation will probably not improve. I'm not sure if she just didn't want to, but sometimes these things aren't easy. Maybe she thought it was weird to have to go to the cemetery, but a lot of magic is weird. However, you have to do what you have to do if you want the payoff. In that particular instance, she needed the help of the ancestors to bring a new ancestor forward into the world.

One final really important thing: don't forget to have sex. If you look at the statistics, most people don't have sex very often. I'm not sure why, but if you are trying to conceive, it goes without saying: have as much sex as possible.

Fertility Oils and Baths

For best results, these fertility oils and baths should be taken by both or all potential parents for maximum success. Please test in advance with a small amount, as you may have sensitivities that you are unaware of. In that case, try something different until you find a formula that resonates with your personal chemistry.

Mating Dance Spell Oil

This spell is designed to play on the complementary energy of two lovers as they join in sacred union. The mating dance is the most important and enjoyable dance we get to do!

INGREDIENTS:
5 drops patchouli oil
5 drops civit oil
5 drops amber oil
¼ ounce sweet almond oil
glass bottle

>> Combine all ingredients in a glass bottle. Bury overnight on the evening of the full moon to charge it with sacred energy. Wear this oil whenever you or your partner are in a sensual union to bring about the most passionate and deep connection possible.

Oshun Fertility Oil

In the religions of New Orleans Voodoo, Santeria (more properly known as La Regla Lucumi), Ifa, Candomblé, and others, the energy and process of fertility are owned by the Orisha Oshun. Some people view her as a goddess, others as a divine manifestation of all that she represents. The are countless legends of her beauty and her assistance for women in need. This formula should be created on the full moon and blessed by washing it in a river. As always, pay attention to your experience as you perform this working. Once I went to the river with Oshun offerings only to find three dead fish; needless to say, the relationship and the working didn't go as planned. Other times I have been blessed with an offering from her in return; once I even found a gold ring. This spell will help bring on the most favorable conditions for pregnancy to occur.

INGREDIENTS:
3 drops orange blossom oil
3 drops amber oil
3 drops myrtle oil
1 small piece citrine crystal
extra-virgin olive oil for base
5 silver or gold coins
glass bottle

>> Combine all ingredients except the coins in a glass bottle. Firmly tighten the top. Then take the bottle to the river. Hold it between your hand and blow on it to infuse it with your energy. Have your partner do the same. Leave the coins in the river. Then gently bathe the bottle in the river water. Wear the formula daily until conception has occurred.

Baby Love Fertility Oil

This is a simple yet effective spell to use when you are trying to conceive a child. It will help alleviate stress and anxiety and focus on the loving creation that is coming.

INGREDIENTS:

¼ ounce grapeseed oil
8 drops geranium oil
2 drops magnolia oil
8 drops neroli oil
glass bottle

>> Combine all ingredients together in a glass bottle. Both potential parents should blow on the bottle to charge it with their breath and intent. Use small amounts on candles or yourself when trying to conceive.

Demeter Fertility Bath

Many of the spells in this book work by honoring and connecting with the energies of ancient goddesses. Here we invoke the sacred power of the Greek goddess Demeter to help with fertility and abundance. Demeter literally means "Earth" and "Mother," and this spell draws on the energy of the Earth to manifest your desire for a child.

INGREDIENTS:
3 drops lavender oil
3 drops jasmine oil
3 drops myrrh oil
1 cup rose water
1 cup orange flower water
large glass jar

>> Combine all ingredients in a large glass jar. Bury in the earth for 24 hours or more in order to receive the blessings of Demeter. Dig up the jar and pour into your bath on the eve of the full moon.

Two Waters Fertility Bath

In the La Regla Lucumi (Santeria) pantheon, Yemaya is the mother of all beings. Together with her sister Oshun, they form the two waters necessary for creation. Women should take this bath on the new moon when they are trying to conceive. It will bring them calm, peace, and the most beneficial conditions for success.

INGREDIENTS:

1 cup ocean water

1 cup river water

1 cup coconut milk

5 drops orange oil

>> Add all ingredients to a warm bath. Absorb the blessing as it washes over your body. Repeat every month as necessary.

Fertility Spells and Powders

The magical spells and formulas in this section will help you improve your potency and hopefully create the best possible circumstances for conception to occur.

Sweet Honey Fertility Jar Spell

Place this spell jar under the center of your bed when you are trying to conceive. It will keep things sweetly flowing in the right direction.

INGREDIENTS:

1 teaspoon cinnamon powder

1 teaspoon nutmeg powder

hair clippings from the potential parents

one jar of honey with comb

>> Add spices and clippings to the jar of honey. Close the jar tight. Place it under your bed and leave it there until your child is born. At that time, you may take the jar and dispose of its contents in running water, such as a stream or ocean.

Fertility Gris-Gris Mix

This spell is most effective when you have this mix both in a bag to be carried in your pocket and also sprinkled under the bed when you are trying to conceive.

INGREDIENTS:
½ cup dried ivy
¼ cup cinnamon, ground
¼ cup dried rose petals
¼ cup dried honeysuckle
¼ cup cloves, ground
¼ cup allspice, ground
pink bag, natural fabric

>> Mix all ingredients together and grind thoroughly with a mortar and pestle. Once the mixture has been made into a fine powder, place some in a natural-fabric pink bag and carry in your pocket. Sprinkle the rest beneath your mattress. Repeat until a baby is on the way!

Plant a Seed Fertility Spell

This crossroads-based spell will help sow the seeds of fertility. It uses grains and seeds and their fertile energies to start these blessings headed your way. This spell is best performed on the full moon. It can be done by one or all partners.

INGREDIENTS:

1 tablespoon sesame seeds
1 tablespoon poppy seeds
1 tablespoon morning glory seeds
1 tablespoon mustard seed
1 tablespoon sunflower seeds
small bowl
½ cup rose water
1 cup tap water

>> Combine the seeds together in a small bowl. Walk to the crossroads nearest your home. Pour out the rose water and the tap water. Sprinkle the seeds and say the following invocation or one of your own choosing: *"These seeds I give to the wind, may blessings follow and grow from within."*

Welcome Back Baby Spell

In the Yoruba language, the names Babatunde and Iyatunde mean "father returns" and "mother returns," respectively. These names are given to infants seen to be the spiritual return, a kind of reincarnation, of an ancestor's spirit. This specific spell is done for new-born infants to help welcome them "back" to their family. The spell's ingredients help bring an infant and its family joy, calm, peace, and if at all possible, a good night's sleep. Please choose large stones for safety purposes.

INGREDIENTS:
white sheet
1 large turquoise crystal
1 large rose quartz crystal
1 large piece obsidian or jet crystal
1 large moonstone crystal
rose water
chamomile tea
spray bottle

≫ Lay the sheet on the floor. Align the crystals as follows: turquoise in the south, rose quartz in the west, jet or obsidian in the north, and moonstone in the east. Put the rose water and the chamomile tea into the spray bottle. Place the baby or something of the baby's (like clothing or a toy) in the center of the sheet. Spray all around the sheet, first walking counterclockwise once and then clockwise once. Pick up the baby or the toys. The crystals can be kept in a safe place for the baby to use when he or she is older.

Geode Charm for Fertility

Geodes, like babies, are a mystery that from the out-side don't look like much. The hidden treasure here, however, is a truly marvelous miracle. This charm should be crafted on the full moon and carried by the mother and/or father throughout the pregnancy.

INGREDIENTS:

glass candle holder

1 white votive candle

1 piece white cloth (natural fabric)

1 small geode

2 drops lavender oil

1 drop myrrh oil

1 drop geranium oil

>> Place the candle holder with a white candle inside on your working altar. Place the white fabric in front of it and place the geode on top. Put one drop of lavender oil on the geode. Place one drop each of lavender oil, myrrh oil, and geranium oil on the candle and light it. When the candle is done burn-ing, dispose of the remains in the trash. Wrap the geode, and from now throughout the pregnancy, the expectant mother should carry it with her in her pocket or bag.

Rabbits, Rabbits, Rabbits
Fertility Pendulum Spell

Rabbits breed very rapidly and are therefore associated in many ways with fertility magic. This spell should be performed on the first day of the month and will help you determine the sex of a baby on the way. Please do your best to obtain rabbit hair or fur from humane sources for the most positive magic possible for both you and the animal. Folklore says you can perform this type of divination with just the parent's wedding ring, but I find this method to be even more effective.

INGREDIENTS:

glass candle holder

1 white votive candle

1 drop lavender oil

9-inch piece of white embroidery floss

ring or other piece of jewelry from the mother

few pieces rabbit hair

≫ Place the candle holder on your working altar. Put the votive candle inside it, place lavender oil on top, and light. Have the expectant mother lie down on her bed. Tie one end of the embroidery floss to the ring and the other to the hair of the hare (pun intended). Ask the pendulum what a girl baby movement will look like, and watch to see how the pendulum responds. Ask the pendulum what a boy baby movement will look like, and watch to see how the pendulum responds. Then hold the pendulum over the mother and ask what the gender of the baby is. Watch carefully to see how the pendulum moves.

Foods for Fertility

What you eat and put into your body is always important, but it takes on a special significance when considering the question of fertility. Everything from shark fin to camel hump has been said to magically help with conception. There are, however, many more mundane foods that will help you increase your fertility, both magically and physically. Focus on the bounty and joy to come while you are preparing these food-based spells and you will truly be blessed.

Dandelion and Rice Soup

This any-season soup includes dandelions, which many think of as a common weed. Dandelions, however, are said to magically impart strength, courage, and the manifestation of wishes. This recipe also includes rice, which is famous for its properties of fertility and prosperity. Dandelion greens are also rich in vitamins A, C, and K. Dandelion blossoms, if you would like to include them as a garnish, should be picked when young to ensure a sweet honey-like taste.

INGREDIENTS:

1 quart vegetable broth
3 cups fresh young dandelion greens,
   picked before the plant has flowered
½ cup white or brown rice
1 teaspoon soy sauce (or soy sauce substitute)
salt and pepper to taste

>> Bring broth to a boil over medium heat. Reduce heat to low and add dandelions. Simmer gently, stirringly occasionally. Add rice and cook covered for ½ hour. Add soy sauce and salt and pepper to taste. Makes 4–5 servings.

Parents' Pesto

The word *pesto* comes from the word *pestare*, which means to pound. The erotic connotations are obvious. A true pesto should be ground in a mortar and pestle, but this version calls for a food processor, a much quicker alternative. The basil in the recipe will help bring healing and focus to your fertility magic, while the pine nuts provide zinc, a necessary nutrient to help overall with male sex drive and libido.

INGREDIENTS:

3 cloves garlic

3 cups basil leaves

¾ cup freshly grated Parmesan cheese

½ cup extra-virgin olive oil

¼ cup pine nuts, lightly toasted

pinch black pepper

≫ Combine all ingredients in a food processor and pulse until completely blended. Enjoy with pasta or as a sauce for chicken or fish.

Sweet Lovers Corn

Corn, as a grain, takes its rightful place as a sacred symbol of fertility. It was, and is still, used by indigenous North and South Americans as a divine component of their everyday lives. Corn comes in many different colors and is said to be ruled by the moon. In addition to providing fertility, it is also said to magically impart protection and luck to those who partake of it wisely, and often you may eat it to gain any of these properties for yourself.

INGREDIENTS:

1 large can creamed corn
1 large can gold and white corn
1 tablespoon sweet butter
1 tablespoon brown sugar
2 tablespoons light cream
salt and pepper to taste

>> Combine all ingredients in a saucepan. Simmer over low heat for 15–20 minutes, stirring frequently. Serve immediately. Makes 5–6 servings.

Chapter Six

UNIVERSAL LOVE SPELLS

The universal love spells in this chapter are designed to salute and honor friends, family, animals, and the wider world around us. I have a dear friend who has been a shamanic practitioner and teacher for many decades. After the end of her marriage, she sat down to perform a love spell for herself. She gathered all the herbs, oils, and magics she needed to manifest her desire. She wrote down all the qualities she desired in a partner. She wrote "kind," "caring," "dedicated," and "faithful." Within a short amount of time, her prayers were answered . . . in the form of a German Shepherd. She had forgotten to write "human." Love does, however, come in all forms, shapes, and sizes. This chapter will help you foster the nonromantic types of love, friendship, and blessing on every level.

Oils and Waters for Love of All Kinds

While the rest of this book focuses on specific romantic-inspired love, these spells are for loving those around you in a platonic way. Here you will find oils for friendship and togetherness.

Fast Friendship Oil

This oil is good when you want to develop new friendships quickly and easily. I like to use it not only for personal gatherings in my home, but also when I am involved in open houses or community events.

INGREDIENTS:

3 drops strawberry oil

3 drops rose oil

3 drops myrrh oil

3 drops bergamot oil

sweet almond oil for base

glass bottle

≫ Place all the ingredients in a small glass bottle. Tighten the lid and throw it gently into the air to bless it with the energy of the universe. Wear this oil whenever you have the possibility of meeting new people.

Best Friends Forever Oil

Some people are lucky enough to have good friends—people who have been there for them through thick and thin, with unselfish support and kindness. This is truly a thing to be grateful for. Perform this ritual with your closest friends to strengthen the trust, caring, and understanding between the two of you. I remember that as a child we used to cement these kinds of bonds with blood by pricking our fingers. This magical pact is a much safer solution for modern times.

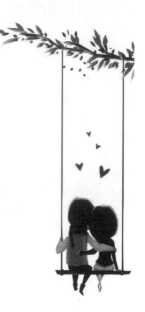

INGREDIENTS:

3 drops copal oil

3 drops orange blossom oil

3 drops amber oil

1 drop peppermint oil

sweet almond oil for base

glass bottle

≫ Combine all ingredients in a glass bottle. Pass the bottle back and forth between you and your friend three times to charge it with your energy. Divide the mixture between you and wear whenever you need to feel the connection the two of you share.

Voodoo Queen Marie Laveau Bath Water

Marie Laveau is the most famous Queen of New Orleans Voodoo. As the first woman to ever hold a public ritual in the United States, her powers are legendary. Up until recently her grave was the second most visited in the country. The archdiocese has now restricted access after an unfortunate incident of vandalism, so the time is ripe for new and different ways of connecting with her. The following formula can be used as a spiritual water for blessing or a bath to be taken on three consecutive nights leading up to the full moon. This formula will help you connect with her energy and improve your powers of divination and command.

INGREDIENTS:
1 tablespoon water from the Mississippi River
1 tablespoon holy water
1 tablespoon spring water
6 drops jasmine oil
6 drops gardenia oil
1 small piece amethyst crystal
glass bottle (large enough to hold amethyst)

>> Combine all ingredients in front of you on your working altar. Place the amethyst in the bottle and then add the rest of the ingredients. Put the top on the bottle. Rub the bottle between your hands to charge it; then gently throw it into the air and catch it. Use the water to cleanse yourself and your home.

Candles and Incense for Universal Love

This section includes fiery candles and incense spells to bring loved ones together, bless your home, and more.

Togetherness Blessing Candle

This candle spell can be performed whenever you are together with loved ones. It will create an atmosphere of community and joy.

INGREDIENTS:

1 white seven-day candle

5 drops frangipani oil

5 drops violet oil

>> Place the oils on the candle. Light and say the following invocation: *"Forces of Earth, Flame, Water, and Wind. Please bless my hearth, my kindred, my friends."*

Home Blessings Candle

Light this candle at home whenever you are getting ready for a ritual or gathering. The candle will remove any negativity and provide a positive atmosphere.

INGREDIENTS:

white votive candle

glass candle holder

3 drops sandalwood oil

3 drops spearmint oil

>> Place the candle in the holder. Add oils to the top and light. Use as often as necessary.

Peaceful Blessings Candle

Maybe you had a stressful day with work or life, and you need a break. Light this candle to connect with peace and truly enjoy some quiet. Be sure to turn off your phone, television, computer, and the rest. This candle will provide you tranquility on all levels.

INGREDIENTS:

glass candle holder

spring water

1 blue votive candle

3 drops lemon oil

3 drops tuberose oil

3 drops myrrh oil

3 drops sweet orange oil

3 drops sandalwood oil

>> Place the candle holder on your working altar. Place a small amount of spring water in the bottom. Put the candle inside the holder and put the oils on top. Light the candle. Breathe deeply and release all the tensions of the day as it burns. Repeat as necessary.

Bob Marley "One Love" Candles

Like most people, I feel a special connection to Bob Marley. Despite his death in 1981, his music and his beautiful message still live on. He spoke of universal love and blessings in many of his songs, and this candle is designed to honor this on every level. It will bring about an atmosphere of inspired bliss and contentment, without the need for additional substances.

INGREDIENTS:
4 candle holders
1 black votive candle
1 red votive candle
1 green votive candle
1 yellow votive candle
4 drops cinnamon oil
4 drops hibiscus oil
4 drops myrrh oil

>> Place the four candle holders on your working altar. Place one candle in each of the four directions. Start by placing the black candle in the north. Next, put the red candle in the south, the green candle in the east,

and the yellow candle in the west. Put one drop of each of the oils onto the candles. Light them starting with the north and moving counterclockwise through the directions. Feel the energy in the room begin to shift as the candles burn down. You may repeat this whenever things become stressful or tense.

Ancestral Connection Candle

Whether we like it or not, sometimes our loved ones have crossed beyond the veil, and we must grieve and connect to them in a different way. This candle is to help you strengthen and understand your communications with the spirit world. Your ancestors are the best place to turn for spiritual help, as they have a stake in your success. Remember their joys and inspiration as you carry out this working. You can use this spell for workings of all kinds.

INGREDIENTS:

small bowl

handful of graveyard dirt (if possible, obtain from the grave of your oldest female ancestor)

1 purple votive candle

3 drops myrrh oil

3 drops lilac oil

dish of your ancestor's favorite food

3 pennies

≫ Place the bowl on your ancestor or working altar and fill with the graveyard dirt. Place the candle in the center of the dirt and put the oils on top. Light the candle. Place the dish of food in front of you. Speak from your heart to your ancestors, telling them your joys and troubles, thanking them for their blessings and love. Place the three pennies into the dirt. When the candle has burned down, please take the dirt and the food outside and leave them under a large tree or at the gates of the cemetery.

Moon Goddess Candle Spell

Many of the spells and rituals call on the energy of the full moon to help charge and bless your creation. This candle spell will help better attune you to the energies of the moon using a piece of moonstone crystal and can be performed at any time. It will allow you to connect with your own emotions and how best to proceed in your specific situation.

INGREDIENTS:

astrological symbol for the moon
1 white seven-day candle
1 blue seven-day candle
2 drops lemon oil
2 drops myrrh oil
2 drops violet oil
1 small piece moonstone

>> Carve the Moon symbol onto both candles. Place one drop each of lemon, myrrh, and violet oil on each candle. Put the small piece of moonstone into the white candle. Light both candles every night until they are burned down. Remove the moonstone and keep it on your working altar.

Earth Healing Candle

One of the most intense public rituals I have ever attended was created with the intent to heal the Earth. As we stood in a circle praying for the betterment of our planet, a figure appeared—a very pregnant woman, veiled and dressed in black. As she traveled among us, she called us out for our misdeeds. "You, in the red shirt, you don't recycle." "And you, over there, what's going on with that compost pile?" This ritualized and direct accountability was very moving, and much more effective than the average empty promise, "fluffy bunny" approach to paganism. This candle spell is designed to help heal the Earth; it can be done solitary or with a group. As with all the spells in this book, I hope you bring to your magic workings both the blessings and responsibility they deserve. Ultimately, we are all responsible to the planet Earth.

INGREDIENTS:

bowl of freshly dug earth

1 green votive candle

1 small piece petrified wood

3 drops lavender oil

3 drops myrrh oil

3 drops oak moss oil

>> Place the bowl outside on the ground, or if this is not possible, put it inside on your working altar. Fill it with the dirt. Place the candle in the center. Put the

piece of petrified wood on top of the dirt in front of the candle. Drip the lavender, myrrh, and oak moss oils onto the top of the candle. Light the candle; then say aloud the promises you will make and keep to help heal the Earth. When the candle has burned down, place the petrified wood on your working altar or carry it in your pocket. The dirt can be disposed of outside under a large tree. This would be a great spell to do for Earth Day or as part of a spring equinox ritual.

Blessings of the Beasts Candle Spell

Traditionally, a blessing of pets is done in the Catholic Church on October 4, the feast day for St. Francis. You can do this spell at that time, or whenever a new pet joins the family. Traditional Wiccans could perform a variation of this for their familiars, or living animal guides, that walk with them. This will help keep them healthy and happy.

1 St. Francis candle or 1 seven-day candle and a
picture of St. Francis underneath

3 drops basil oil

3 drops carnation oil

>> Place the oils on the candle and light. Say the
following prayer or one of your own choosing:
*"St. Francis, we ask your blessing for the creatures
that we love, that you shine on them and bring them
health and well-being."* If you prefer, you may use
the traditional Catholic blessing for this occasion
instead, which usually includes a variation of Psalm
148; it includes puppies, guppies, and all animals
in between.

Tourmaline Threshold Spell

Black tourmaline is a wonderfully magical crystal
best used for removing negativity and protection. This
spell will help bless and protect your home by setting
up a sacred line of protection at your threshold. Use
this whenever you need your defenses strengthened.

INGREDIENTS:

2 small pieces black tourmaline

holy water

2 drops sandalwood oil

>> Wash the crystals in holy water. Place one drop of
sandalwood oil on each and place them on either

side of the entrance to your home. This way, when people cross your threshold, they will do so with the best of energies and intentions. Repeat every few months to keep your home protected.

Animal Love and Healing Spell

The reason for many of the calls I receive from clients is that they need spells to help heal a sick animal. Anyone who has an animal knows that pets are like our children: they depend on us for their survival and care in every way. When they are sick, sometimes traditional medicine is at a loss for a solution, so this spell may help provide some relief. Use it whenever you think your animals might need some assistance.

Note: Usually, in these situations, I make it a point to pray for the best possible outcome. No one man nor beast can live forever, even with the best magic and medicine available.

INGREDIENTS:
1 cup spring water
1 cup holy water
glass candle holder
1 white votive candle
3 drops myrrh oil
3 drops sandalwood oil
1 drop colloidal silver

personal item from the animal (this can be hair, nail
   clippings, shed snakeskin, etc.)
white cloth
large bowl

>> Place the waters in the bottom of a large bowl. Place
the candle holder in the center of the bowl, and then
place the votive candle inside the bowl. Put the oils
on top of the candle and light it. Place the silver and
personal item into the bowl. When the candle has
burned down, you may remove it and dispose of it in
the trash or under a large tree. Dip the corner of the
white cloth into the water and use this to wipe down
your animal or the animal's cage/habitat. Repeat as
needed.

Sweet Not Sour Lemon Spell

This simple folk magic spell is designed for friendship. Use it whenever you are getting together with new friends.

INGREDIENTS:
slices of lemon

>> Place a slice of lemon under a new friend's chair to help secure the friendship. After the friend has left, dispose of the slice outside under a large tree or bush.

To All My Friends Spell

Traditionally, many Norse rituals involve a segment that in modern times is referred to as the "oath, boast, toast." Friends gather together around a large table and take turns making oaths about the coming years, boasts about their skills, and toasts to their loved ones. For this working, you will need a bunch of good friends, a bottle, and the following items. This spell working will help strengthen your community and ensure its success.

INGREDIENTS:

glass candle holder
purple votive candle
3 drops rosemary oil
3 drops orange blossom oil
long piece of red cord
bottle of liquor or other appropriate beverage

>> Place the candle holder in the center of the table where everyone is going to sit. Place the oils on the candle in the holder and light it. Tie the cord around the bottle, pass the bottle around, and begin your words. As each person takes a turn, tie a knot in the string and pass it along until both are done. Bury the bottle outside, and remember to always keep true to your words with your deeds.

Fairy Blessings Herbal Spell

Most adult practitioners of magic learn very quickly that fairies are in reality very different from the way our childhood selves imagined them. Fairies are expert at making things look much better than they really are, in "looking on the bright side," if you will. This candle spell will help you see everything in its most positive light. Use whenever you need a better outlook on your situation.

INGREDIENTS:

food and drink offering for the fairies
5 tea light candles
5 pinches meadowsweet herb, dried
5 pinches sweet woodruff herb, dried
5 pinches violet blossoms, dried
gold glitter

>> Leave the fairy food and drink outside under a large tree or in a fairy ring, if you are lucky enough to have one nearby. Go inside your home and place the candles on your working altar. Add one pinch each of the meadowsweet, sweet woodruff, and violet to each candle, along with a dash of glitter. Next, light each of the five candles in a different place in your home or yard. Be sure you place them safely and do not leave unattended. As these candles burn, an atmosphere of beautiful positivity will burn as well.

Universal Love Vision Board Spell

A vision board is a collage of images and words designed to inspire and focus your energy. It could include photos of your patron goddesses, gods, or symbols of your tradition. It could include sacred words, chants, or prayers. It can also include things you want or desire in your life. Let your creativity flow; there is absolutely no end to the possibilities. This idea could also be expanded and applied as you create a vision box or scrapbook—see where your mind and your spirit take you. You can use this spell to manifest your desires in love or any other area you wish.

INGREDIENTS OR ELEMENTS:
white candle
1 drop lavender oil
glue
photos or images of the things you want in your life
posterboard or box to attach them to
your imagination

>> Light the candle to help clear your mind and focus your energy. Place the lavender oil in your glue and stir. Next, start cutting out the pictures and gluing them to the board. Think of all the wonderful new blessings that will be coming into your life. Put the board or box someplace where you will see it frequently.

Lonely No More Spell

This spell will help you gain more friends and alleviate loneliness. It uses a candle, oils, and a psalm to help you achieve your goals. In addition to the psalm, feel free to use any words of positive invocation as part of this working. Use this spell to achieve a more active social life.

INGREDIENTS:

1 yellow votive candle
glass candle holder
5 drops frangipani oil
5 drops magnolia oil
5 drops lavender oil
Psalm 133

>> Place the candle holder in the center of your working altar. Put the yellow candle in the holder and put the frangipani, magnolia, and lavender oils, on the candle and light it. Take a deep breath. Take another. Say Psalm 133 or an invocation of your own. This spell can be performed at any time and is especially effective for gatherings and holidays.

Silent Supper Spell

Many pagan groups eat a "Dumb Supper" in silence for ancestors as part of Samhain festivities. This spell will show you how to set up the table, and the meal that you choose to eat should be based on the favorite foods of the loved ones you are honoring in this way. This is more a spell of honoring than manifestation, but if you are lucky, your ancestors will grant you success in all areas of your life.

INGREDIENTS:

1 white tablecloth
4 purple votive candles

4 drops cypress oil
4 drops lavender oil
4 drops myrrh oil
2 (or more) white dishes
food for the ancestors
drink for the ancestors
small bell

>> Lay the tablecloth out on your dining table or altar. Place one candle in each of the four directions. Onto each candle, place one drop each of cypress, lavender, and myrrh oil. Place a serving of food on one of the white plates and put it in the center of the table. Place a drink there for the ancestors too. Ring the bell. Light the candles. Say the following prayer or one of your own choosing.

> *"I eat in silence to honor thee*
> *and I remember your joy,*
> *and I remember your lessons taught me.*
> *And how a blissful future you employ."*

- You may now make a plate for yourself and any others taking part. The food should be eaten in complete silence. This ritual is best performed on the full moon closest to Samhain, also known as Halloween.

God/Goddess Box Spell

There may be a time when you have exhausted all options in a situation and you have to give it over to God, Goddess, or the universe for the proper solution. This concept will be familiar to those involved in twelve-step programs or fellowships, where participants frequently let the universe sort out things that are beyond their control. I remember once asking a woman who had been in one of these programs for over two decades if she had a "God Box." When she replied yes, I asked her what she had put in it over the years. She said she honestly couldn't remember; those problems were removed from her mind and her life. This spell will help you make your own box to give those troubles over to a higher authority, be it Goddess, God, or the universe. It is great when you have run out of solutions and need a different approach.

INGREDIENTS:

1 box

decorations for box (paint, photos, etc.)

2 pieces quartz crystal

2 pieces selenite crystal

4 drops sandalwood oil

>> Begin by decorating your box however you please; use images and elements that inspire you and make you feel attached to the divine. Place the box on your working altar. Open the box and place the crystals inside in the four corners. Put one drop of sandalwood oil on each of the crystals. The next time you

have a problem that seems insurmountable, write it on a piece of paper and put it in the box. That problem is now in the hands of the universe, so do your best to not stress or fret about it anymore and trust that the outcome will be for the best. Use this spell whenever you feel the need.

Hold On to Happiness Incense

Burn this incense on charcoal discs or throw on the campfire whenever you are having a good time and want to have more. This will create an atmosphere of great joy.

INGREDIENTS:
½ cup red rose petals, dried
5 drops frangipani oil
5 drops jasmine oil
1 tablespoon amber resin
ceramic bowl
charcoal discs

>> Combine roses, oils, and resin in the bowl. Mix well with your hands, using gloves if necessary. Burn on charcoal.

Foods to Celebrate Universal Love

Sharing food with your loved ones on holidays or any day can be a great way to connect with them. There is no reason you can't highlight and increase the magical blessings of these meals.

Blossom Salad

This salad salutes all kinds of love. The blossoms will give loving blessings to the eater. Arugula is an aphrodisiac and is called natural Viagra by some. Make this salad often to bring caring and passion to those who eat it, and always remember to share the love.

INGREDIENTS:

1 cup arugula, washed, dried, and prepared for salad

2 cups romaine lettuce greens, washed, dried, and prepared for salad

1 cup baby spinach greens, washed, dried, and prepared for salad

¼ cup black olives, pitted and sliced

2 tablespoons basil flowers

6 nasturtium blossoms
6 chive blossoms
¼ cup red onion, diced (optional)
1 tomato, chopped
¼ cup chopped red pepper
¼ cup shredded carrots
¼ cup sunflower seeds, hulled

>> Combine all ingredients in a large salad bowl and toss well to combine. Serve with a red wine vinaigrette or other salad dressing. This recipe serves 2–3 as a main course or 4–5 as a side salad.

Winter Wassail Recipe

Anyone who comes to my home during the Yuletide season receives a cup of wassail. Many are familiar with the holiday carol "Here We Come A-wassailing," but they are unsure what the drink actually is. The word *wassail* literally translates to "good health," and this delicious brew is designed to bring healing blessings to you and your loved ones. This recipe will help foster the health of your own spiritual family.

INGREDIENTS:
1 gallon apple cider
3 oranges, sliced with seeds removed
½ cup orange juice
¼ cup lemon juice
5 cinnamon sticks

>> Combine all ingredients in a large pot on the stove. Simmer over very low heat for 10–15 minutes, stirring occasionally. Serve warm.

Roasted Sweet Potatoes for the Ancestors

Ancestors first, last, and always is one of my mottoes. While I was writing my *African-American Ritual Cookbook*, I almost titled it *101 Things to Do with Sweet Potatoes*. So many ancestors' recipes involve these delicious roots, including this one. Cook this dish to bring ancestor blessings into all areas of your life—financial, personal, and spiritual. It will also help you honor and salute the ancestors' wisdom and carry on their traditions.

INGREDIENTS:

2 tablespoons maple syrup
4 tablespoons sweet butter, melted
1 tablespoon lime juice

3 cups cooked, mashed sweet potatoes
¼ cup chopped almonds
¼ cup chopped pecans

>> Add maple syrup, butter, and juice to sweet pota-
toes and stir to combine. Place in a shallow baking
dish and top with chopped nuts. Bake sweet potatoes in a 350-degree oven for 20–25 minutes or until
the top begins to brown slightly.

Chapter Seven

SPELLS FOR LOVE ... ACTUALLY

There is always how people want love to unfold, and then there is love ... actually. Unfortunately, many of us have to deal with problems like divorce, infidelity, jealousy, sexually transmitted disease, and other unpleasantness. As always, seek medical, legal, or other necessary advice in addition to any spiritual solutions you are looking to implement. There are several reasons why the spells you may be doing to find love, romance, passion, and the like may not have the desired results. Honestly, this isn't my favorite list. I am also not fond of the list of reasons I can't eat candy all day or people don't live forever.

Reasons You Might Not Be Successful in Your Love Workings

Maybe something better is around the corner.

Maybe you are not ready for the necessary changes that would be taking place in your life.

Maybe you are looking in the wrong place.

Maybe something or someone is standing in your way.

Maybe there is another reason; this is why divination is so important. If you can't perform divination successfully for yourself (and some people struggle with this), look to find someone to do a reading or consultation for you.

In my magical practice, I have had plenty of people come to me for spells to bring back lost love. Most of the time they don't really have the means or, more importantly, desire to complete the spell they are looking for. They will call me up a week later and tell me they are in love with someone else, or they will expect back a different lover than they let go of in the first place. I had an ex-boyfriend who used to do tattoos; he told me he once was asked to cover up every name he had ever inked on a client. Like it or not, all relationships end in death or breakup; those are the only options we have. It is important to seriously consider if moving on or past the situation wouldn't be more pleasant than having the lover back. Making people do something they don't want to do, especially where love and sex are concerned, may not be the best choice and could be quite dubious and unfair. A love spell is not the same as consent.

That said, there are spells in this chapter that will help you get back or get rid of a lost lover or spouse, get rid of an interfering party, and remove jealousy.

Oils, Waters, and Washes for Love . . . Actually

While writing this chapter about waters and washes, I thought about including a spell that was a big bottle of liquor with a "Drink Me" tag, like something out of *Alice in Wonderland*. Not that I would ever advocate substance abuse, but there are many different ways to wash someone out of your life. There are ways to keep them in it too, and everything in between.

Baby Come Back Oil

This oil is designed to make a lost love return to you if at all possible. You can use it if you know their location or even if you have completely lost touch with them. Please be sure this is what you want, as this working is easier to complete than it is to undo.

INGREDIENTS:

3 drops galangal oil
3 drops vetivert oil
3 drops myrrh oil
½ ounce sweet almond oil
glass bottle
small piece of lodestone
sample of your lost love's handwriting

>> Place all the oils together in a glass bottle. Add the lodestone. Tear the handwriting into small pieces and place them in the bottle too. Wear this oil whenever you are going to see, speak, or search for your lost love.

Up and Over Oil

This oil will soothe a broken heart and help you to lift yourself back up after a relationship doesn't turn out as desired. Use it as soon as possible after a breakup.

INGREDIENTS:

3 drops carnation oil
3 drops rose oil
3 drops sunflower oil
3 drops gardenia oil
¼ ounce sweet almond oil
glass bottle

>> Combine oils in a glass bottle. Make the sign of the crossroads with the bottle to charge it. Wear the oil as often as necessary.

Jealousy Gone Oil

This oil is designed to help remove feelings of jealousy and replace them with confidence. Use this oil spell if you are feeling insecure or uncertain about your situation.

INGREDIENTS:
3 drops Roman chamomile oil
3 drops frankincense oil
3 drops lavender oil
½ ounce sweet almond oil
glass bottle

>> Blend oils together in a small glass bottle. Throw it gently into the air to consecrate it. Wear or sprinkle the oil about the home as needed.

All's Fair Oil

The age-old saying has it that "all is fair in love and war." This magical oil is designed to help you get fairness and equality in your relationships. It combines traditional botanicals for improving communication and receiving clarity and justice. Use it when you need a truthful and honest answer to your problems.

INGREDIENTS:

3 drops basil oil
3 drops sandalwood oil
3 drops lavender oil
3 drops Dittany of Crete oil
½ ounce sweet almond oil
glass bottle

>> Combine all ingredients in a glass bottle. Take a deep breath and exhale onto the bottle. Bury the bottle underground for 24 hours to charge it with the energy of the Earth. Use the oil whenever you are to see or speak to your partner to bring about best results.

Get Rid of Gossip Oil

Gossip never helps anything. Some people, however, seem to have nothing better to do than to keep their eyes, ears, nose, and tongue in other people's business. Haters are going to hate, but this oil will help shut their mouths about it. Use this to halt gossip and negativity in all forms.

INGREDIENTS:

6 drops clove oil
6 drops sage oil
6 drops sandalwood oil
¼ ounce sweet almond oil
glass bottle

>> Place all the ingredients together into a glass bottle. Throw it gently into the air to charge the bottle with the energy of the invisibles. Wear the oil whenever you feel that the words of others are affecting you in a bad way.

Commanding, Compelling, Controlling Oil

This oil recipe is directly designed to influence others and make them do your will. The energies of this spell are dark—and not in a good way. It is best crafted during the full moon to take advantage of the drawing energies of this time. It is difficult to predict what else will change when using this spell, so please proceed with caution. This can alter things drastically.

INGREDIENTS:
3 drops bayberry oil
2 drops copal oil
2 drops patchouli oil
½ ounce sweet almond oil
glass bottle

>> Mix all ingredients together in a small glass bottle. Rub it between your hands to charge it. Wear the oil whenever you are going to come in contact with the person you are attempting to compel.

St. Jude Water to Manifest the Impossible

Hoodoo magic relies heavily on the power of the saints. St. Jude is the patron saint of the impossible. New Orleans is famous for its international shrine of St. Jude. The last time I visited the city, I stopped by only to find that they were out of holy water at the time. I was disappointed, to say the least. I must have been making a sad face because just then the janitor turned the corner and offered to send me some in the mail. I happily gave him a few dollars for postage and was sure he would forget. I received my own St. Jude miracle when a month later a package complete with two full bottles of holy water showed up at my home in New York City. With St. Jude, all things can be possible. Use this spell in your own life when you are praying and waiting for a miracle. It can bring amazing results in a short amount of time.

INGREDIENTS:

4 ounces holy water
6 drops frankincense oil
6 drops basil oil
glass bottle

≫ Combine ingredients together in a bottle. Make the sign of the cross in the air with the bottle. Sprinkle the water about your home or space whenever you wish for some serious and speedy change.

Three Is Not Company Floor Wash

Some people choose to be in relationships with multiple people, and if you are polyamorous and it works as a lifestyle choice for you, I applaud your choice. However, many people find themselves in situations in which there is an extra person that not everyone agrees to or is necessarily happy about. In these cases, there are spells that you can use to remove this person from the romance. This spell has two parts: one must be completed outside the home, and the other inside its walls. This floor wash will protect what you have and keep outsiders away from your partnership.

INGREDIENTS:

1 white bowl

2 cups spring water

1 cup holy water

3 drops sandalwood oil

3 drops rose oil

3 drops orange oil

1 small white candle

1 black bowl

3 drops rosemary oil

3 drops black pepper oil

spit (I promise I will explain)

>> Take the white bowl and fill with 1 cup spring water, 1 cup holy water, sandalwood oil, rose oil, and orange oil. Place the white candle in the center of the bowl and light it. Next, take the black bowl, and in it place 1 cup spring water, rosemary oil, black pepper oil. Then spit in the mixture when you are done. Walk around the outside of your home counterclockwise sprinkling the water. Try not to get any on yourself. When you have done your best to go around the house in a full circle, go back into your home. Take the white bowl and extinguish the candle, saying the words *"Although I extinguish you, may your power shine forever."* Remove the candle from the bowl. Take the remaining water and use it to wash the corners of your home and your windows. If you like, you can add some tap water and also wash the floors. Repeat the floor wash monthly or until the situation has improved.

Stay Here Floor Wash

This spell is designed to keep someone from leaving. It can keep a reluctant lover or partner in place. Use with caution and be careful that is really what you want.

INGREDIENTS:

1 gallon tap water

piece of fabric torn from the clothing of the person you wish to have stay

3 drops clove oil

3 drops sage oil

3 ounces Florida water

≫ Mix all items together in a clean bucket. On the full moon, use the mixture to wash your floors, windows, and doors. Repeat every full moon or as necessary.

Run Devil Run Bath

As a rule, I don't believe in the existence of simple binaries like good versus evil, God versus the Devil, and the like, but in my many years of magic, often I have come across dark and dangerous forces. Like it or not, rats, roaches, and psychotic maniacs exist. If people find themselves in contact with negative forces, one thing that they can do is take this cleansing bath for three consecutive nights starting on the new moon. This will provide serious and powerful energies for protection.

INGREDIENTS:

1 tablespoon grains of paradise

1 ounce espanta muerto (botanical name *Eclipta Prostrata*), fresh herb

1 cup spring water

1 dash holy water

¼ cup bay rum cologne

6 drops myrrh oil

6 drops basil oil

≫ Combine all dry ingredients in a large glass jar. Boil spring water on the stove and then remove from heat. Add the holy water and bay rum and then pour the whole mix slowly over the herbs and oils. Leave the mixture on the windowsill or outside for 24 hours where it will charge with both the sun's and the moon's rays. Strain. Divide into three portions and pour one over you each night in the tub for three consecutive nights. As an added note, do not create this formula on Good Friday, as the Catholic tradition believes this is the day when the devil is allowed to walk among us. Even though I don't go in for others' superstitions, it's probably best not to tempt fate. In many Santeria (more correctly known as La Regla Lucumi) houses, no spiritual work is done at all during Holy Week, from Palm Sunday to Easter Sunday.

Spells and Herbs for Love Gone Mad, Bad, or Dangerous to Know

These spells incorporate many different ways to deal with love that is not going the way you intended.

Fidelity Jar Spell

This spell is created to keep someone faithful within the boundaries of a committed relationship. It has the necessary ingredients to foster an affectionate, truthful, and sincere connection between partners. The effectiveness of this spell jar increases with the use of personal items from the people involved.

INGREDIENTS:

3 drops nutmeg oil

3 drops clove oil

¼ ounce dried myrtle

¼ ounce dried clover

personal items (hair, piece of clothing, nail clippings, etc.)

½ full honey jar (taste it first)

>> Combine all ingredients in the honey jar and shake well. Place under the center of the bed you share with your partner.

Mine, Mine, Mine Gris-Gris Bag

This formula can be done as a promise of fidelity between two people or by one person to strengthen the fidelity of a partner. You can guess which one is easier. This formula contains traditional herbs and oils to help you keep to the bonds of your relationship.

INGREDIENTS:
½ ounce dried ivy
10 drops myrtle oil
5 drops carnation oil
small black natural-fabric bag

>> Combine ingredients together on the night of the full moon. Wear daily or sprinkle about the bedroom every full moon.

Ring My Bell Gris-Gris for Your Phone

Staring at the phone won't make it ring. I know; I have tried. Techno-magic makes new and interesting strides every day with the advent of new technology. This spell employs some old techniques to some new tools to help you start talking.

I have a good but peculiar friend who was staying at my house once. He was working for a bunch of designers during Fashion Week, so he was keeping interesting hours. I keep interesting hours too, and I woke very early one morning to find him putting some money and his phone on my ancestor altar. I didn't think much of it, but I asked him later what was going on. He replied simply that he was "fixing his phone." "Did it work?" I replied. "Of course," he said. Now you don't have to perform this spell on your ancestor altar; your working altar will do just fine. Use this spell to bring about speedy communication between partners.

INGREDIENTS:

medium-size bowl
¼ cup dill, dried
¼ cup basil, dried
¼ cup thyme, dried
¼ cup mugwort, dried
3 drops vanilla oil

>> Place the bowl on your working altar. Combine all ingredients into the bowl and mix together well with your hands. Place your phone on the center of the altar, and around it moving clockwise, spread the herbs in a circle. Leave the phone there inside the circle for 1 hour. You should hear from the person within 24 to 36 hours if not sooner; otherwise, consider performing some divination or another type of spell.

Erzulie Freda Spell

This spell is to heal from disappointments in love. Erzulie Freda is the Haitian Lwa of love; most images show her crying over her lost loves and for people who don't live up to being their best selves. She is associated with the color pink, and very often people represent her with images of the Virgin Mary. Use this spell when you are feeling helpless or are courting some cosmic compassion.

INGREDIENTS:

1 bunch of white grapes

1 medium-sized piece of white lace

6 white flowers—roses, daisies, or the like

>> Take the above items to a waterfall. Lay out the lace on the ground and place the grapes in the center. Remove the flowers from their stems and bathe each one in the water. As you do this, feel the negativity release itself from your life. Place the flowers one at a time into the lace. Tie up the cloth and throw into the waterfall. Turn around and don't look back.

Tie It Down Spell

This spell is designed to keep a man faithful. It also comes with one of the funniest love-spell stories ever. A former friend was using this spell on a person she was dating. He was not used to magic and would not have been pleased that she was using it on him. Customarily, with these types of spells, it is best if they are not detected by the other person, which tends to neutralize the working or worse. My friend found herself on a packed train traveling to a hot date with the cord still tied to her waist. She knew if she arrived with it still on, he would detect it. She then tried to saw it off through her clothing with her keys (they were all she had) while she was on the phone with me. It pays to think ahead with any spellwork before you find yourself in a difficult situation. Use this spell to keep your partner incapable of performing sexually with anyone but you. As always, proceed with caution.

INGREDIENTS:

red cord long enough to tie around your waist
myrtle oil

>> Anoint the two ends of the cord with myrtle oil. Now for the hard part: measure your partner's member with the cord. Double and triple the cord back over itself until it becomes long enough to go around your waist once and tie. Cut off the excess cord and bury at the crossroads. Wear the cord at all times, except when it could be discovered. At that point, discard and create another if necessary.

Breakup Barbie Doll Spell

Modern witches are crafty. While many choose to go the traditional route when making a doll for sympathetic magic and use natural cloth, some have chosen to substitute Barbie dolls to do the work for them. Choose a doll with the same physical features as the person you are working on, if at all possible. In this spell, you will be trying to directly affect people to make a different choice than the one they are currently making. Having as many of their personal items as possible is very important for your success. Use this spell to separate two people who are in a relationship.

INGREDIENTS:

1 male or female doll to represent the person you are working on

1 male or female doll to represent the other person
   you are working on
personal items from the people you are working on
   (clothes, hair, signature, photo, etc.)
1 pinch black pepper
1 pinch red pepper
1 pinch cat hair
1 pinch dog hair
1 shoebox

>> For the first doll you are working with, attach the
   full birth name of the person and the personal
   items you have collected with glue. Repeat with the
   other doll. Lay the dolls in front of you on your altar
   space, making sure they are near to each other but
   not touching. In between the two dolls, place the
   peppers and hairs. Move the dolls farther apart and
   state out loud what you would like to happen in the
   situation and why. For example, *"May these two be
   separated. . . ."*

   • Next comes the creative part: if one of the dolls
     represents someone you would like to stay close
     to, take that doll and bury it as close as possible
     to your property. If you are unable to do this, get
     a large plant pot, fill it with dirt, the doll, and a
     houseplant. Be sure to take good care of it, and
     do your best to make sure it is not discovered, for
     that will require you to start the entire spell over

again. If you are not attached to one of the parties, leave the doll under a large tree in a local park or wooded area. Take the other doll and put it in the box with the hair and peppers. Take the box to your nearest bus station or train station and put it in the trash there. This symbolizes the person leaving you and the other party alone, and getting out of your way.

Hoodoo Spell to Rid Yourself of an Enemy

Love can sometimes be tainted by jealousy or envy from petty outsiders. Use this spell employing traditional Hoodoo methods to remove an enemy from your life. It will help that person stay away for good. Many Hoodoo spells uses psalms or other bible passages to help manifest their magic. If this makes you uncomfortable, consider trying a different tactic or spell.

INGREDIENTS:

3 coins
1 white tea light candle
Psalm 70 (see Appendix A)
personal item or the name of
    enemy written on parchment
    paper
brown paper bag

>> Place all the items in front on your working altar. Light the tea light candle and say Psalm 70 (you can use the version in the appendix or a different one, if you prefer). When the candle has burned out, place the remains of the candle along with the coins and personal item into the bag. Take the bag to the river or ocean and drop it in. Turn away and do not look back. The person should remove himself or herself from your life fairly quickly.

Incense, Candles, and Herbal Spells for Love in Actuality

Unfortunately, not all love looks like that in a cinematic fairy tale. People can be dishonest or unfair when it comes to love. These magical workings may help you make things more comfortable, improve communication, and also learn the truth about a situation. You may use them for any or all of these circumstances.

Catfish Reveal Incense

The modern era presents some interesting challenges. Like it or not, the people we love may not be who they claim to be. Thanks to the popular tv show of the same name, the word *catfish* recently had another definition added to the dictionary: it now also means someone who disguises himself or herself on the Internet or otherwise for purposes of love. Use this spell to receive honest information about your romance.

INGREDIENTS:
3 drops basil oil
pinch of mugwort
1 teaspoon sandalwood tears
1 disc self-lighting charcoal incense

>> Mix the oil and other ingredients together. Burn on charcoal in a well-ventilated area before you are about to communicate with the person you wish to learn the truth about. Be thoroughly prepared for whatever it is you find.

Simbi Communication Candle

In the tradition of Haitian Vodou, Simbi is the Lwa, or honored energy, responsible for communication and magic. Many times in a relationship that is experiencing difficulty, communication has broken down between lovers, and very little can be done under those circumstances. Charge up this candle to improve communication between you and your love when things seem almost hopeless. It is especially useful when people are not even speaking at all.

INGREDIENTS:

veve for Simbi or astrological symbol for Mercury
green seven-day candle in glass
3 copper pennies
pinch lodestone
3 drops basil oil

>> Draw the symbol or veve on the candle with a marker.
Place the candle on your working altar and surround
it with the three pennies. Add the pinch of lodestone
and the basil oil. Light the candle for seven nights in
a row, extinguishing it each night before you go to
bed. While you are putting it out, envision the chan-
nels of contact opening up between you and your
partner. After the seven nights are over, leave the
candle under a large tree.

Long Distance Lonely Candle

Work, family, and life often separate us from those
we love. This candle spell is designed to strengthen
you while you and your loved ones are apart. It will
help give you happiness and solutions for these difficult times.

INGREDIENTS:

1 white votive candle
glass candle holder
6 drops lavender oil
6 drops frangipani oil

>> Place the candle in the holder and cover with the oils. Light the candle, and as it burns, concentrate on past and future good times with your love. Remember to breathe deeply and focus your mind as the candle burns. Repeat as necessary.

Obsession Be Gone Candle

In the worst of circumstances, it can be difficult to have the strength to let go of love. The mind keeps bringing you back. Once that relationship has passed, every delicious thought of love can turn to pain, and for a desperate few, this pain can become an obsession. People can become truly powerless over love and sex, and for them, I recommend investigating a twelve-step program. There are several love and/or sex fellowships. I have spent time in those recovery rooms, and two of the most valuable things they provide are solutions and faith. The prayer that accompanies this spell is a modified version of a prayer from those rooms. This spell is very useful in overcoming obsession of all kinds.

INGREDIENTS:
1 black votive candle
1 white votive candle
2 glass candle holders
3 pennies
2 pinches black salt
2 drops myrrh oil

2 drops lavender oil

2 drops basil oil

obsession prayer or prayer of your own choosing

>> Place all ingredients onto your working altar. Place the candles in the holders—the white to your right side, the black candle to your left. Place the pennies in the center and cover with the black salt. Put one drop each of the myrrh, lavender, and basil oils on each candle. Say the following prayer or one of your own, *"God, Goddess, or Higher Power, please remove this unnecessary obsession from me and replace it with the thoughts, feelings, and deeds of who you wish me to be."* When the candles have burned down, take the pennies and throw over your left shoulder into the nearest crossroads. Do not look behind you.

Truth Will Come Out Incense

Burn this incense when you need lovers or others to be honest and tell the truth. Light incense on charcoal on the eve of the full moon for best results. It will reveal secrets from every possible place.

INGREDIENTS:

2 drops bayberry oil

2 drops cedarwood oil

¼ cup dried rosemary

¼ cup dried sage

charcoal discs

>> Combine the first four ingredients in a mortar and pestle and mix thoroughly. Burn on charcoal discs whenever truth, honesty, and insight are required.

Spells for Love Actually

As you can tell from this book so far, love can be a dirty business. First and foremost, I recommend trying all traditional methods to improve the situation before resorting to magic. As one of my mentors is wont to illustrate, sometimes a slap is quicker than a spell. I don't advocate violence, and almost never would, but the first question that comes to mind in these instances when people come to me for spellwork is "Would you step on an insect that was in your living room?" Unwanted influences must be dealt with, and these spells will give you a variety of ways to accomplish this successfully.

A Note about Menstrual Magic: This type of working can be very intense. Cultures from Native America to Africa hold taboos against menstruating women performing magic or using their blood as part of a working. That said, there are binding spells to incorporate these energies. Use your best judgment, as always.

Ice Princess Freezer Spell

When you need to stop someone from continuing bad behavior, this is the spell to use. It puts the person in a "frozen" state, and that person is unable to continue objectionable ways. Use it to quickly freeze people in their tracks.

INGREDIENTS:

personal item from the person you are doing the working on (hair, signature, or the like)
small glass jar
pinch black pepper
2 drops bayberry oil
2 drops pine oil
tap water

>> This spell is best performed on the waning moon. Place the personal item into the glass jar. Cover with the pepper, bayberry oil, and pine oil. Fill the jar with

tap water almost to the rim. Place the jar in the freezer until the contents are frozen solid. Leave it there until it is no longer needed (the individual isn't a problem anymore); then dispose of it under a large tree.

Rock Hard Crystal Spell

Pagans traditionally utilize crystals for grounding and connecting to the Earth. Earth magic helps one to feel centered, establish a firm foundation, and put down roots. Sometimes after a breakup or just when you're having difficulty, it is hard to feel stable and productive. This spell will help improve that and allow you to get your bearings again.

INGREDIENTS:

glass candle holder
tap water
1 white votive candle
4 onyx or jet crystals
5 drops sandalwood oil
5 drops myrrh oil
5 drops cedarwood oil

>> Place the candle holder on your working altar. Place a small amount of tap water in the bottom of the glass. Put the candle on top. Place the crystals around the candle—one in each of the four directions. Add the oils. Light the candle and concentrate on your new foundation for the future.

Gone and Away Spell

The purpose of this spell is to make someone leave your home and your life for good. It usually works fast, and the person will not be troubling you again. Please be sure this is exactly what you desire before performing the spell.

INGREDIENTS:
Florida water
pinch sea salt
the broom from the house
fork

>> Sprinkle a small amount of Florida water behind the main entrance to the home. Then sprinkle salt in the same place. Next, turn the broom upside down behind the door with the bristles pointing upward. Jab the fork into the broom. The offending person should leave quickly.

Downfall of Social Media Spell

A lot of good and bad can be said about the reality of social media. Even some of my friends and family have had affairs and other issues come up as a result of being on social media, and when you find yourself in one of

these negative circumstances, you need solutions. This spell is an extreme solution, so before using it, you would be wise to consult divination and other options first. It will bring serious negativity onto an individual and keep that person down.

INGREDIENTS:
small printout/photo of the person you are
    trying to rid yourself of
pinch of black pepper
pinch of white pepper
pinch of red pepper
pinch of rue

>> Write the name of the person you are trying to remove from your life on the back of the picture. Tear the picture into nine small pieces, ball each one up, and throw them into the toilet. Throw the peppers and the rue into the toilet too. Now, I apologize in advance if I'm going to offend you with the next statement, but pee on the mixture and flush. As the items go down the toilet, concentrate on the person leaving for good. This spell can be used to prevent cyberbullying.

Burning Bed Spell

Do not bring a bed from an old relationship into a new one. This spell doesn't really burn a whole bed. But your old bed can hold the memories, thoughts, experiences, and energy from your past relationship. I repeat: do not bring these with you into your new life. If your past situation was particularly negative, you may wish to perform this spell to release that energy when you get rid of the bed. It will help you let go of any old ties. Be sure to bless the new bed too with some happiness oil or gris-gris herbal mixture.

INGREDIENTS:
1 dash holy water
1 dash tap water
glass candle holder
piece of fabric cut from the mattress
1 black votive candle
3 drops carnation oil
3 drops cedarwood oil

>> Place the waters in the bottom of the candle holder. Put the small amount of fabric in the water and place the candle on top. Put the carnation and cedarwood oil on top. Light the candle and imagine all the bad memories from the relationship washing away from your life. Breathe deeply as the candle burns. Say the following words or use those of your own choosing: *"As you burn, please release from me all that was not truly meant to be."* As always, never leave a burning candle unattended. When the candle is done, you can dispose of the remains in the trash.

Chapter Eight

LOVE AND SEX RITES AND RITUALS

The most successful magic happens with increase. While some situations may be solved by lighting a candle or wearing an oil, more intense transformations can occur when putting several of these elements together as part of a larger rite or rituals. Beginners or newcomers to magical practice might feel more comfortable starting with something smaller, but people should not be afraid to expand their practice into something larger.

In this chapter you will find ways to craft your spells together to manifest your desires. These spells can be performed alone or, if you like, with others to help you bring the joys of love and sex into your life. Just about any of the spells included in this book can be incorporated into larger rituals, and I hope your creative mind and magical body do so often, but here are a few to get you started.

One, Two, Three, Go . . .
Beginnings of Love Ritual

The start of a relationship can be slow going occasionally, and you may find it in your best interest to perform a ritual to help the love affair get off to a healthy start. This formula will attract loving blessings to your new union. Perform this ritual on the eve of the full moon. For the ingredients listed, you can use the formulas found in this book or purchase commercially made ones. It has been my experience that when you are completing a major working, it is helpful to obtain magical ingredients from other practitioners occasionally. Everyone has different skills, and most of the time the more help you can get, the better. Consider trading with another spiritual person so you can both benefit from each other's talents.

INGREDIENTS:
3 pink votive candles
3 glass candle holders

spring water
Oshun bath

>> Place the candles on your working altar in the holders. Pour a small amount of spring water in each. Light them and concentrate on your desires. Now it is time to take the Oshun bath. Focus on your ideal love manifesting in your life.

Arabian Nights Ritual

One of the most famous love stories of all time is the *The Arabian Nights*, also known as *One Thousand and One Arabian Nights*. The history of the story is almost a history of eroticism itself. Sir Richard Francis Burton's translation scandalized Victorian England in the 1880s. The United States had its own banned version that made the rounds in the 1920s. So what was all the fuss about the tales? They are ancient Arabian tales, supposedly told by Scheherazade to her husband, King Shariar, each night to avoid her death. This ritual will help bring that kind of enthralling passion and love into your life physically, spiritually, and emotionally.

INGREDIENTS:

rose quartz water

altar set up in the southern part of your bedroom or home

symbol for love (this can be a heart or a rune such as Kenaz or Wunjo)

river water
red plate or bowl
3 red votive candles
ring of fire oil
drunken Oshun oranges (see recipe in Chapter Four)

>> Spray the rose quartz water in all the corners of your home, paying particular attention to your bedroom and altar space. Carve the symbol for love onto the candles with a ritual knife or quill. Place a small amount of river water in the plate or bowl and place the candles on top. Say the following prayer or use one of your own:

> *"Scheherazade from tales of old,*
> *help me craft my love story as a joy to behold."*

• Place a drop of the ring of fire oil on each candle and light them. Eat some drunken oranges alone or share with your lover. Let the candles burn down and wear the oil each time you and your lover are to come together.

Elysian Fields Ritual

In Greek and Roman lore, the Elysian fields were a place of paradise, a resting place for the gods and goddesses where all was bliss. This ritual is not to be confused with Aleister Crowley's Rites of Eleusis, which he performed in London in 1910. This specific ritual is designed to artfully craft a magical place and space to bring about your blissful dreams of erotic pleasure. Breathe deeply and feel the changes in your body and your space as this spell unfolds to manifest your most sensual desires.

INGREDIENTS:

Happiness bath (found in Chapter One)

red altar cloth

1 seven-color seven-day candle

marinated olives (recipe in Chapter Three)

3 drops rose oil

3 drops jasmine oil

3 drops gardenia oil

1 drop lemongrass oil

» The night before you perform this ritual, you and the other ritualists should take the Happiness bath. Next, choose a room for the ritual. It can be a bedroom or a living room, but in any case, make sure you have a large area to work with. Set up a table in the center of the room to use as your working altar. Cover with the red altar cloth. Place the candle on the altar. Place the olives on the altar in front of the candle. Add the jasmine, gardenia, lemongrass, and rose oil to the candle and light it. Sit around the altar table, and as the candle burns, share the olives and your visions of past and future happiness. When you have eaten all the olives, extinguish the candle with these words: *"Even though I extinguish you, may your fires of joy and happiness shine forever."* You can light the candle again whenever you need to create a space of divine happiness.

Bells on Vision Quest Ritual

Childhood is, and should be, a magical time. One of my favorite rhymes from childhood is, some historians believe, about Queen Elizabeth I, whereas others think it is actually about a more magical journey with the Lady of the Lake, the one we will be honoring here. This ritual will help you find your path to supreme joy.

INGREDIENTS:

white clothing
¼ cup lake water
1 small bowl
1 amethyst crystal
1 quartz crystal
1 white votive candle
3 drops sandalwood oil
3 drops thyme oil
1 small bell

>> Assemble all items on your working altar. Dress yourself in white clothing. Pour the lake water into the bowl and put the amethyst and quartz crystal into the water. Put the votive candle in the center of the bowl. Place the sandalwood and thyme oils on the top of the candle and light it. Ring the bell. As the candle burns, do your best to breathe deeply and

remain open to the images and thoughts that present themselves to you. Recite the following, probably familiar, rhyme:

> *"Ride a cock horse*
> *to Banbury Cross*
> *to see a fine lady*
> *upon a white horse*
> *rings on her fingers*
> *and bells on her toes,*
> *she shall have music*
> *wherever she goes."*

>> When the candle has burned out, remove the crystals and place them under your bed. You are at a crossroads and will dream of your new beginnings to come.

New Beginnings Tarot Ritual

Tarot is one of the most effective tools that practitioners have for learning about their future and the world around them. While many use it for divination, it is also highly effective when used symbolically as part of a larger ritual. Perform this ritual at the start of any new undertaking: the beginning of a sacred circle or group, the start of a new relationship, the beginning a new job, or whenever you feel a new change coming.

INGREDIENTS:
cascarilla
1 white sheet

1 Fool tarot card, from your preferred tarot deck
4 white seven-day candles
1 Palo Santo stick
1 recipe Fool's eggs (found in chapter one)
1 white bucket or basin
1 gallon spring water
1 cup white rose petals
1 cup Kolonia con Sandalo (with sandalwood) cologne

>> Have each of the ritual participants take off their shoes and draw a cross on the bottom of their feet with the cascarilla. Spread the sheet out on the floor. Place the tarot card in the center. In each of the directions, place a white candle. Light the Palo Santo stick and move throughout your space counterclockwise, paying special attention to corners and windows. Eat the eggs, sharing with the others participating. Next, place the bucket in the center of the sheet on top of the tarot card. Fill the bucket with the water, rose petals, and Kolonia. Next, each of the participants in the ritual will step forward and take turns washing their hands in the water, saying aloud their wishes for new beginnings. When everyone has done this, have the last person take the mixture outside and dump out at the nearest crossroads. Put out the candles with these words: *"Though I extinguish you now, may our new beginnings bloom forever."* All the group members may bring a candle home and light whenever they need to feel inspired blessings and strength in their life.

Love and Lapis Ritual

This ritual is focused around fostering love of all kinds. It uses lapis lazuli, the legendary blue stone, for spiritual power and love. Simply touching your body with lapis lazuli is believed to bring about feelings of peace and joy. Sumerian lovers Inanna and Dumuzi are legendary, and lapis lazuli is said to have been central to their passions. This ritual honors them and is best performed with two or more people on the full moon. It will salute and honor the deep and holy connection that can and should occur between lovers.

INGREDIENTS:
Black Cat Bast oil (from Chapter Two)
1 blue votive candle
glass candle holder
3 drops lavender oil
1 jar honey
1 piece of lapis lazuli for each
    participant (can be a stone or pendant)

>> Begin by having all the ritualists place the Bast oil on their wrists, neck, and other pulse points. Place the blue candle in the holder and light it. Drop the lavender oil into the jar of honey and taste the mix. Pass the lapis lazuli crystals across the flame and then dip gently into the honey. Lick the honey from the stone. From this moment forward, wear or carry the stone with you to bring divine love and blessings.

Protect from the Ex Ritual

Unfortunately, many people find themselves in difficult and dangerous situations with ex-spouses, lovers, and the like. Please SEEK HELP from the authorities, police, or your local domestic abuse shelter if necessary. There are, however, times when spellwork is still needed to separate yourself from your ex, and this ritual will help you to do that. Before doing this, be sure all the other items belonging to the person are out of your home. You may place them in a garbage bag outside if necessary. I remember once doing this when my godmother and I got to this part in the discussion, and she asked me if all my boyfriend's stuff was gone and in the garbage. I replied, "I put it in a bag." "What kind of bag?" she asked. "A recycling bag," I answered. Clearly, I had a different and more recycling-based agenda for the future. Be sure a separation is truly what you want before proceeding. This spell will remove your ex from your life physically and emotionally.

INGREDIENTS:

personal item from your ex (handwriting, clothing, etc.)
1 piece onyx
Florida water
Psalm 44 (see Appendix A)

>> Bring all the items to the crossroads nearest your home. Place the personal item on the ground (you

can also bury it if you prefer), place the onyx on top, and sprinkle with Florida water. Say Psalm 44. Turn around, leaving the items (except the water), and do not look back. When you return home, cleanse your hands and feet with the Florida water.

Give Back to the Earth Ritual

Humans have only one planet to live on, and the Earth is it. Unfortunately, it has been polluted and disrespected almost since the beginning of humankind. This solitary or group ritual is designed to reconnect you to the Earth while giving back to the planet by planting a tree. All too often I have been to what I refer to as "Whirled Peas" (World Peace) Healing Earth rituals that raise little energy and effect even less change. This ritual gives you something concrete to do to help the Earth. This would be a particularly good ritual to do for a natural or man-made disaster, times when our minds and hearts are especially focused on the supreme importance of nature.

INGREDIENTS:
brown candle
1 small citrine quartz crystal
¼ cup frankincense tears
1 large spoonful of dirt
1 small tree for planting
1 cup holy water

>> Prepare and light the brown candle on your working altar. Place the citrine quartz crystal and the frankincense on the dirt. When the candle has burned down, take the dirt, contents, and the tree outside to the place you have chosen for planting. Dig your hole, and place the dirt and its additions into the bottom of the hole. Then plant the tree in the hole. Water with the holy water and additional tap water as necessary. Continue to care for your tree as best you can in the days, months, and years to come. It is representative of your connection to the Earth.

Chapter Nine

MATERIA MAGICA

agical herbs and ingredients can vary between name or variety, depending on location, folklore, or the practices of the individual. Whenever possible, I have attempted to give you both the botanical name and folk names for the more unusual items. Some people may have questions about using substitutions. Yes, substitutions are possible, like using cinnamon sticks instead of cinnamon oil, but whenever possible, try to obtain the listed ingredients for best results.

Decades ago when I first started learning and practicing magic, it was very difficult to find some of the necessary items. If practitioners were lucky, they had one store to go to, and they made the pilgrimage regularly. Nowadays people have a lot more options for buying and finding out about magical items. I still encourage you to support your local pagan store. Many of these people work hard to provide knowledgeable services and items for their community, and they need your patronage. That said, many who are reading this may live in isolated communities far from any like-minded individuals or stores; in that case, you can find many of these ingredients online.

Sacred Herbs and Botanicals

Abre camino (*Eupatorium villosum, Trichilia havanensis*)—This herb is used commonly in La Regla Lucumi, also known as Santeria or Ocha, to help alleviate difficulties in all areas of life. Most often it is used as a floor wash or bath, but it is also grown around the home for protection and success.

Allspice (*Pimenta dioica, Pimenta officinalis*)—Allspice is not really "all spices" at all, but rather the berry of an evergreen tree. Aphrodite and Venus are two goddesses associated with this spice. It is helpful with fertility issues, healing, compassion, and all aspects of love.

Apple (*Malus pumila*)—Sacred apples aren't just for the Bible. Actually, their delicious magical history is as old as their cultivation itself. They are aphrodisiacs and lend blessings to any magic regarding the emotions or love. They are also used in divination and harvest spells and workings.

Apple blossom (*Pyrus coronaria*)—These blossoms lend special blessings of love. They produce feelings of deep romantic and devoted love.

Basil (*Ocimum basilicum*)—Basil was a holy herb not only for the Romans but also for Eastern cultures. Myth has it that you are to curse while sowing the seeds; this will invoke the plant's natural property of dispelling demons. Magically, it will lend protection and help exorcise any demons.

Bayberry (*Myrica*)—Used primarily to remove curses and to draw money, bayberry can also be added to love spells to make wishes come true and improve your clarity.

Bay leaf (*Laurus nobilis*)—Many people use bay leaves in all types of magic. No self-respecting kitchen witch should go without them. You can use the leaves to write the name of your lover, or your friend, and use it to bless both them and your relationship. You can even grow a bay leaf tree for protection magic and a fresh supply in your own home.

Bergamot (*Citrus bergamia*)—Bergamot is a classic ingredient in high-end perfumes and blends, and its citrus scent has many magical uses, including love and joy. You can add this to just about any magical spell to improve your chances of success.

Bloodroot (*Sanguinaria canadensis*)—The bloodroot plant has amazing white blossoms; it was used traditionally by Native Americans. It can be used in your marriage magic for protecting and strengthening a relationship. Wrap it in a red cloth and carry it to attract love in all forms. The plant juices can be toxic, so use caution.

Cardamom (*Elettaria cardamomum*)—This is another delightful kitchen spice. In your spells, it will bring romance, joy, and energy to the situation. Ruled by the planet Venus, cardamom is also reported to help with your libido.

Carnation (*Dianthus caryophyllus*)—Carnations, even in the garden, stand tall, proud, and ruffly, like they are floral royalty. Magically, they are said to bring on blessings of love and healing.

Cedarwood (*Cedrus spp.*)—In aromatherapy, cedarwood is used to bring about feelings of calm and to alleviate anxiety. Cedarwood oil in your magic will help bring protective blessings. Its energy is said to be incorruptible. Some Norse practitioners use it to honor the god Odin.

Chamomile, German (*Matricaria chamomilla*)—The tiny yellow flowers of the chamomile are said to contain the power to help with insomnia, luck, protection, and gentle love. It is also frequently associated with children and fairy magics.

Cinnamon (*Cinnamomum zeylanicum*)—Cinnamon heats things up, and love and sex are no exception; it's the rule. Many say cinnamon is ruled by the sun, and it can also help with healing and also improving your psychic powers.

Civit—Civit is a precious perfume ingredient made from the anal glands of the civit cat. Like most animal magics, it can add a powerful lust and abandon to your magic. It works to stimulate the Root chakra and can be helpful when you're working on this area. Please be mindful that many animals today are being treated inhumanely to obtain this ingredient, and synthetic formulas are available. As always, please shop and spellcraft responsibly.

Cloves (*Eugenia caryophyllata*)—Cloves are an important spice to have in your kitchen cupboard and in your magical stockpile as well. When worn or carried, they are said to stop people from gossiping about you. In the La Regla Lucumi tradition, cloves are sacred to the Orisha Oshun, whose domain is love.

Coffee grounds (*Coffea arabica*)—Coffee can be used for divination, but it can also be used in your magic for literally "waking" up your spells and workings. In the New Orleans Voodoo tradition and La Regla Lucumi, it is used as a regular offering to help open the way to success.

Copal (*Protium copal*)—This is Egyptian magic for healing. It is great for inviting in the energy of the sun. It is used primarily in Central America to protect and bless.

Cypress (*Cupressus sempervirens*)—This swampy plant is used to bring Earth blessings, healing, and wealth. Cypress oil is also used in protection magic.

Daisy (*Chrysanthemum leucanthemum*)—Folklore associates the simple daisy with love and divination. Questioning lovers are said to pull the petals from a daisy, reciting the words "they love me, they love me not," as a simple divination to determine the outcome of a love situation. Daisies can also be used in your love magic to bring truth and romantic devotion to your workings.

Dandelion (*Taraxacum officinale*)—Unfortunately, many magical traditions are lost to us nowadays; happily, this is not the case with dandelions. Even small children know that you can wish upon a dandelion seed pod to send your desires out to the universe.

Dill (*Anethum graveolens*)—Dill is an herb of protection, blessing, and communication. Even some wedding brooms are crafted from dill stalks.

Dittany of Crete (*Origanum Dictamnus*)—A member of the mint family, this herb grows wild on the island of Crete. It is used for love, astral projection, and manifestation of your desires.

Dove's blood oil—Legend says that at one time this came from an actual dove; nowadays it is made from herbs and resins soaked in oil and/or ink. Many psychic workings call for this oil to actually write or anoint written spells and to fortify and manifest your magics.

Dragon's blood (*Dracaena draco, Croton lechleri*)—Sorry to disappoint, but this is not made from legitimate dragons. Dragon's blood is made of the dried resin of a species of Croton or Dracaena tree. I have seen it used in formulas for banishing, purging your space of negativity, developing courage, and providing protection. Dragon's blood oil and incense are also said to activate the Crown chakra.

Espanta Muerto (*Eclipta Prostrata*)—Also known as tattoo plant, this herb is used in the Lucumi tradition to remove jinxes, curses, and bad spirits. Most often it is used as a bath or floor wash. It is most easily obtained online or from your local botanica.

Frankincense (*Boswellia carterii*)—Frankincense has been used for thousands of years for blessings, protection, psychic connection, and sacred ceremonies. Traditionally, frankincense was said to be most effective when burned in the morning. For the spells in this book, you can use the oil or the dried resin, which is called tears. Red-colored frankincense is harvested in the spring. If possible, use this type for your spells involving passion and sex.

Frangipani (*Plumeria rubra*)—The frangipani flower is sweet and exotic. Also known as *Plumeria* or templetree, it has magical energies that bring a sweet and happy love.

Freesia (*Freesia alba, Freesia fucata*, etc.)—Said to heal and open the Heart chakra, freesia is an intoxicating scent that should be used often. It is also a traditional anniversary flower and can be used to bring trust and a friendly atmosphere to any situation.

Galangal (*Alpinia officinarum*)—Galangal, which is also called Little John (or Little John to chew), is used in magic for power, protection, and spells of increase.

Gardenia (*Gardenia spp.*)—This flower has a sweet and delightful scent that brings pleasure and romance to your spellcrafting. Its white color makes it a frequent addition to traditional wedding bouquets, where it represents divine purity.

Ginger (*Zingiber officinale*)—Ginger is another kitchen herb that you can use in your love and sex magics to liven things up. This herb is also used in Asian medicine for healing. Primarily, it gives heat in your recipes and in your magic.

Grains of paradise (*Amomum melegueta*)—Also called Guinea pepper or alligator pepper, this spicy little pepper can be used in divination, power, and lust magic. Some spells call for putting them in your mouth and spitting them about the room, while others just have you keep them in your pocket.

Heliotrope (*Heliotropium peruviana*)—In the Victorian language of flowers, this delicate purple beauty was said to signify devotion in a relationship. It can bring peace, calm, and joy to your spells.

Honeysuckle (*Lonicera spp.*)—A delicate wedding flower, it is used to bring sweetness and affection to your union. The blossoms themselves are even edible, and the oil can be used in your spellcrafting.

Hibiscus (*Hibiscus spp.*)—In the islands, hibiscus is known as Jamaica flower. In your love magic, it will bring simple love, peace, and joy. Hibiscus is also helpful in chakra balancing.

High John the Conqueror root (*Ipomoea Jalapa*)— A relative of common morning glory, this wrinkly root is used in Hoodoo, Voodoo, and Southern Rootworking for everything from justice to love spells. Its proper botanical name stems from Xalapa, Mexico, where it grows in abundance.

Jasmine (*Jasminum officinale*)—Love and happiness are the qualities of jasmine. Adding this to your love magics will help you gain sincerity and grace in your relationships. It can also help with attracting beneficial spirits.

Juniper (*Juniperus communis*)—The berries of the juniper bush can be used in spells for luck and love. It is also a common ingredient in gin. The scent is strong and unusual, so use sparingly.

Lavender (*Lavandula angustifolia*)—This all-purpose beauty is a standard in many gardens and should be a standard in your magical cabinet too. It functions primarily as an amplifier and will give a boost to almost any working. Lavender is also used frequently in protection magics, and is both calming and stimulating.

Lemon (*Citrus limonum*)—Lemon is said to bring clarity and psychic protection. You can use it in your magic for romantic love and friendship.

Lilac (*Syringa vulgaris*)—Fragrant and beautiful, this flower is full of love blessings. Its purple blooms entice truthfulness and a pure heart.

Lily (*Lilium spp.*)—Customarily a flower of remembrance, lily can also bring beauty and joy to your working. The delicate flower is said to be ruled by the goddesses Venus and Juno, making it useful for many different types of love and marriage spellcrafting. When carried just picked from the garden, it is reported to protect you from negative love magics being performed against you.

Lily of the valley (*Convallaria majalis*)—This tiny white bell-shaped flower is believed to bring happiness and a positive outlook to your workings.

Lime (*Citrus spp.*)—Lime is used to strengthen spellwork and to bring about friendship. It is also useful in spells for protection and spiritual cleansing.

Lotus (*Nelumbo nucifera*)—Lotus is used to connect with all the higher realms. It connects all your thoughts and focus to the divine.

Magnolia (*Magnolia spp.*)—This sweet Southern beauty will bring love blessings and joy your way. In the Victorian language of flowers, it meant perseverance. Use it in your magic for a devoted and blissful relationship.

Marigold (*Calendula officinalis*)—A Hindu wedding flower, this common garden ornament can bring about special blessings of love.

Meadowsweet (*Filipendula ulmaria*)—This hardy herb has many medicinal as well as magical uses. In your spellwork, it will bring a special blessing to weddings, as its alternate name is bridewort. Meadowsweet is also reported to bring about great joy, healing, and happiness.

Mugwort (*Artemisia vulgaris*)—This herb vibrates with the energy of the moon. It's very helpful when trying to improve your psychic abilities and in astral travel.

Musk—Originally, this oil came from the sex glands of animals themselves; these days most of what is sold in stores is synthetic but carries the primal energy of its namesake.

Myrrh (*Commiphora myrrha*)—Sacred to the goddesses Isis and Hecate, myrrh is not really an herb, but technically a resin that comes from a tree grown in parts of northern Africa. Myrrh is harvested by cutting slices into the bark, which then drips out the golden resin, commonly referred to as tears. These tears are used as an incense base for many different magical formulas. Myrrh is considered feminine and is associated primarily with the energy of the moon. Myrrh is said to activate both the Base and the Crown chakras.

Myrtle (*Myrtus communis*)—Myrtle flowers are traditionally used in fidelity magic. Use the oil or herb in your workings for dedication and faithfulness in your relationship.

Neroli, orange blossom (*Citrus aurantium*)—Oil of neroli is made from the flowers of the bitter orange. Its wildly floral scent is exotic and sweet and can be used in both romantic and sexual magic spells.

Nutmeg (*Myristica fragrans*)—Nutmeg can be intoxicating; even science has proven that in large quantities it can be both toxic and psychedelic. In your magic, it will bring love and a sultry passion to the table. Nutmeg can also be used to ensure fidelity in a relationship.

Orange, sweet (*Citrus aurantium dulcis*)—When I was little, my Nana always told me how she and her sister got an orange in their stocking for Christmas when they were little. Oranges are indeed a precious gift. In the La Regla Lucumi tradition, they are a standard offering for the Orisha Oshun, whose domain is sweet honey love.

Orchid (*Orchis spp.*)—This beautiful and delicate flower has often been used in love and sex magic. Some may be surprised to find out that actually vanilla bean comes from a species of orchid.

Orris root (*Iris germanica*)—Orris is actually the root of the iris plant. Used primarily as a fixative in commercial perfumery, it finds its way into many love spells as an ingredient for both passion and faithful promises.

Palo Santo (*Bursera graveolens*)—Palo Santo has both spiritual and scientific uses. This marvelous stick is used in many different traditions in Central America and throughout the world. The botanical species is related to the sacred herb frankincense, but it is native to Peru and Ecuador. Its power of protection is so strong that it is even said to repel flies and mosquitoes. You can put it in your magic to bless, protect, and remove negativity. I like to use it for public blessings and ceremonies because it is much safer than sage for people who may be pregnant or suffering from sensitivities.

Passion flower (*Passiflora spp.*)—This tropical flower is useful in love magic for bringing passion and warm friendship to your life. There are hundreds of flowers identified as passion flower or passion vine that are classified under the genus *Passiflora*.

Patchouli (*Pogostemon cablin*)—An exotic herb of lusty passion, it is used for hot nights of sexual delight. It was once a hippie standard. Use sparingly, as its fragrance is powerful.

Peony (*Paeonia spp.*)—This traditional wedding flower is used for bridal bouquets to bring happiness. It is also said to dispel negativity.

Peppermint (*Mentha piperita*)—Energizing, healing, and protective mint is one of the most common herbs around. In your garden it will grow like a weed, but it will also cross-pollinate if there are any other mint plants in the vicinity.

Pine (*Pinus spp.*)—This cleansing and healing herb also brings quick success. Both pine needles and pine oil can be used in your spells.

Poppy seed (*Papaver spp.*)—Just like in *The Wizard of Oz*, poppies are known to bring sleep and prophetic dreams. In love magic, they are used for romance and fertility. They have the benefit of also being edible and can be used in your magical recipes for the table.

Rose (*Rosa spp.*)—If there is one flower that everyone associates with love, it is the rose. Throughout time it has meant romance, love, devotion, passion, and more. Practitioners can use the oil, petals, or wood in their magic.

Rosemary (*Rosmarinus officinalis*)—Used for both weddings and funerals, rosemary is one of the most versatile herbs around. I have seen both wreaths and crowns made from rosemary.

Rose of Jericho (*Selaginella lepidophylla*)—Rose of Jericho is also known as resurrection plant; when you put it into water, it comes back to life. It can be used in magic to return a situation to its former glory. Most often people add change to revitalize their finances, or beans and herbs to renew their health.

Rosewood (*Rosa spp.*)—Rosewood is highly nourishing and spiritual in its vibration. Use it in your ritual and magic to bring about compassion, love, grace, and healing.

Rue (*Ruta graveolens*)—Over the ages rue has been used for curses, hexes, and protection. Even the word itself means to curse or regret, as in the phrase "you will rue the day."

Sage (*Salvia officinalis*)—Sage is healing, cleansing, and blessing. Pregnant women and nursing mothers should avoid this herb.

Sandalwood (*Santalum album*)—Sandalwood is another scent that is cross-culturally used for divine blessings and protection. Its harmonizing energies are very often associated with the element of water.

Sesame (*Sesamum indicum*)—The simple seeds on the top of your sandwich roll are sporting some powerful magic. Both sesame seed and sesame oil are used to stimulate your Root and Heart chakras. It will bring devoted love and intense passion to your spells.

Spearmint (*Mentha spicata*)—Spearmint, like the other mints, is great for banishing and protection. In particular, this is used in the Lucumi tradition for the Orisha Yemaya, the mother of the ocean. Simply smelling it is said to increase your psychic connections. Either the herb or the oil can be used in your magics.

Strawberry (*Fragaria ananassa*)—Strawberries with their sensual shape and delicious taste have long been used for love magic and blessing. They lend an atmosphere of joy and bliss to your spells.

Sunflower (*Helianthus annuus*)—Bright and shiny like the sun itself, sunflowers lend the qualities of joy, healing, and adoration to your love spells. They are also said to foster loyalty and truthfulness in all situations, and folklore has it that simply eating them will make you much more fertile.

Sweet pea (*Lathyrus odoratus*)—One of the earliest flowers of spring, this delicate beauty can be used in your magic for harmony, friendship, and courage.

Thyme (*Thymus vulgaris*)—This kitchen herb is said to bring courage, protection, health, loyalty, and affection. You can use it in your meals or your magic to bring about longevity in all that you do.

Tuberose (*Polianthes tuberosa*)—Delicate and divinely sensual, this flower will bring an air of joy and bliss to your magic.

Vervain (*Verbena officinalis*)—In the Hoodoo tradition, this herb is used for protection and also aphrodisiac magic. The scent is strong and earthy, so test to your liking before you use it in spellcraft.

Violet (*Viola odorata*)—Delicate purple flowers that volunteer in many a garden, violets can be used in your magic for a happy, affectionate, and faithful love.

Vanilla (*Vanilla planifolia*)—Vanilla is obtained from a species of orchid flower grown in exotic climates. It can be used in both your edible and nonedible magic. It has the power to calm, and also to bring love and passionate joy to your life.

Woodruff (*Asperula odorata*)—Sweet woodruff has been connected to love throughout history. It is a main ingredient in May wine, which is drunk on Beltane to bring fertile blessings for the coming year. The plant is found growing wild along the banks of the Rhine River in Europe. I have grown this herb in my own garden, and it is hardy and beautiful.

Yarrow (*Achillea millefolium*)—Yarrow stalks, often used in divination, are also associated with love. These tall flowers are related to Queen Anne's Lace and do indeed look regal. Some associate it with the goddess Freya.

Ylang Ylang (*Cananga odorata*)—Ylang ylang is one of the most common ingredients used in love potions and perfumes. It brings on sensuality, erotic passion, and dreamy love.

Sacred Waters

Bay rum—This cologne has been used since Victorian times. One whiff and its strong scent brings back memories of earlier times. Use for protection and sacred blessing magics.

Florida water—Florida water is not really a water at all, but rather a perfume blend consisting of several different florals in an alcohol base. The blend has been in use for over two hundred years in countries as diverse as Peru to Surinam. In my personal experience, commercial preparations are more useful in ritual than homemade formulas. This blend functions as an all-purpose amplifier and blessing water useful in almost any situation.

Holy water—Holy water, either from a Catholic Church or from a sacred site, is often used for blessings and divine protection.

May rainwater—Rain collected during the month of May is said to contain the energy of Beltane, or May Day, the pagan holiday when the Earth is teeming with new life and possibility. It was a time for feasts, celebrations, marriages, maypoles, dancing, and much joy.

Orange flower water—This commercial preparation contains botanicals including orange blossoms and others. You can also make your own orange flower water by adding a few drops of neroli, or orange blossom oil, to some spring water.

Spring water—Spring water wells up from deep in the Earth. Use it in your magical spells and workings to bring about both grounding and a new start. Sometimes in my spells I will use exotic spring water from a tropical island or a foreign country. Feel free to do this too if the spirit moves you.

Tap water—Many of the spells in this book call for the addition of tap water. This isn't out of laziness; tap water runs under the Earth from its origins right to your faucet. It will help with your magic of manifestation and also give your spells an element of place, namely yours.

Sacred Crystals

Amber—Amber is ancient dried plant resin. Just the thought of it is magical. Over time the liquid transforms into a solid. Magically, it vibrates with the energy of the sun. Energetically, it is electric and will actually hold a charge when rubbed with silk or wool. It can therefore be used to literally charge up your spellwork and bring happiness and joy to your endeavors.

Amethyst—Amethyst is part of the quartz family. It is used as an all-purpose stone, lending energy and psychic power to all that it does. It vibrates with purity, love, and healing.

Carnelian—Carnelian glows with its sunny powers of healing. In many ways, it reminds me of fire but in a rock form. Ancient Egyptians believed the stone helped to quell feelings of anger and jealousy. You can carry it when you are ready to heal from a past relationship, or in any of the formulas in this book that call for it.

Citrine—This orange stone of healing and passion is said to help manifest your desires in great abundance. It can be used to help clear your Sacral chakra.

Garnet—This deep red stone of love and energy will activate your Root chakra and bless your relationship. Originally, this crystal was used in engagement rings, instead of diamonds, to represent love.

Lodestone—Lodestone functions as a natural magnet. Place it in your magic spells and on your altar to draw your desires and wishes to you and to attract beneficial energies to all that you do.

Quartz crystal—Quartz crystal is probably the most commonly used magical stone. It will bring protection, peace, calm, and healing, and it can also be used to recharge any of the chakras. It enhances wisdom and spiritual connection. Quartz is a crystal that you can use as an all-around power stone.

Rose quartz—This crystal, like many of the other forms of quartz mentioned in the book, is a catalyst for love. Because it is associated with the Heart chakra, you can even buy these crystals shaped in a heart form.

Selenite—Selenite has become popular lately as a stone that can connect you with the divine. It resonates with the Crown chakra. Selenite is useful for removing obstacles and negativity. It is also believed to reunite lovers for a common goal.

Sunstone—Magically, Sunstone is said to be healing and pacifying, and it will remove psychic vampires, just like the sun itself. It can be used with the Root and Sacral chakras to help heal past trauma and energize. A few different stones are identified as sunstone, so find one that resonates with you and your specific energy.

Turquoise—Many Native American traditions use turquoise as a sacred stone for love and healing as it is believed to connect one with the Great Mother. It vibrates with an energy of peace and watery bliss. You can use it in connection with the Throat and Heart chakras. Folklore says that turquoise was formed from the bones of those who died from love.

Unakite—Unakite has been called the "couples" stone and can be used for romantic magic and also spells of self-love, calm, and confidence. The stone is, in reality, a fusion of different stones: jasper, feldspar, epidote, and quartz. It can be carried or used in rituals involving sacred geometry to help your working literally come together like the stone.

* ACKNOWLEDGMENTS *

Many thanks and heartfelt blessings to Nia and Aria Dorsey, Grace Buterbaugh, Priestess Miriam Chamani, Gros Mambo Bonnie Devlin, Ochun Olukari Al'aye, Ogbe Di, Tehron Gillis, Christian, Michele, Vincent, Victoria, Tish, Glenn, Mel, Dot, Amanda, Jenn, Cat, all my godbrothers and godsisters, my loving family, Liam Nadeau, Phoenyx Precil, Samuel Visnic, the Esoterico Brooklyn Collective, Bellavia, Athena Dugan, Risa Sharpe, Elizabeth Koelle, Mishlen Linden, Louis Martinie, Daniella Waterhawk, Heather Killen, Bruce Baker, Isaac Bonewits, Crystal Blanton, Morganna Davies, Jason Winslade, Diana Paxson, Tom Schneider, Witchdoctor Utu and the Dragon Ritual Drummers, Dr. John—aka Mac Rebennack, St. Expedite, and my honored ancestors.

THE PSALMS

Psalm 17

1 Hear the right, O Lord, attend unto my cry, give ear
   unto my prayer, that goeth not out of feigned lips.

2 Let my sentence come forth from thy presence;
   let thine eyes behold the things that are equal.

3 Thou hast proved mine heart; thou hast visited me in the night; thou hast tried me, and shalt find nothing; I am purposed that my mouth shall not transgress.

4 Concerning the works of men, by the word of thy lips I have kept me from the paths of the destroyer.

5 Hold up my goings in thy paths, that my footsteps slip not.

6 I have called upon thee, for thou wilt hear me, O God: incline thine ear unto me, and hear my speech.

7 Show thy marvelous lovingkindness, O thou that savest by thy right hand them which put their trust in thee from those that rise up against them.

8 Keep me as the apple of the eye, hide me under the shadow of thy wings,

9 From the wicked that oppress me, from my deadly enemies, who compass me about.

10 They are inclosed in their own fat: with their mouth they speak proudly.

11 They have now compassed us in our steps: they have set their eyes bowing down to the earth;

12 Like as a lion that is greedy of his prey, and as it were a young lion lurking in secret places.

13 Arise, O Lord, disappoint him, cast him down: deliver my soul from the wicked, which is thy sword:

14 From men which are thy hand, O Lord, from men of the world, which have their portion in this life, and whose belly thou fillest with thy hid treasure: they are full of children, and leave the rest of their substance to their babes.

15 As for me, I will behold thy face in righteousness: I shall be satisfied, when I awake, with thy likeness.

—King James Bible

Psalm 44

1 We have heard with our ears, O God, our fathers have told us, what work thou didst in their days, in the times of old.

2 How thou didst drive out the heathen with thy hand, and plantedst them; how thou didst afflict the people, and cast them out.

3 For they got not the land in possession by their own sword, neither did their own arm save them: but thy right hand, and thine arm, and the light of thy countenance, because thou hadst a favour unto them.

4 Thou art my King, O God: command deliverances for Jacob.

5 Through thee will we push down our enemies: through thy name will we tread them under that rise up against us.

6 For I will not trust in my bow, neither shall my sword save me.

7 But thou hast saved us from our enemies, and hast put them to shame that hated us.

8 In God we boast all the day long, and praise thy name for ever. Selah.

9 But thou hast cast off, and put us to shame; and goest not forth with our armies.

10 Thou makest us to turn back from the enemy: and they which hate us spoil for themselves.

11 Thou hast given us like sheep appointed for meat; and hast scattered us among the heathen.

12 Thou sellest thy people for nought, and dost not increase thy wealth by their price.

13 Thou makest us a reproach to our neighbours, a scorn and a derision to them that are round about us.

14 Thou makest us a byword among the heathen, a shaking of the head among the people.

15 My confusion is continually before me, and the shame of my face hath covered me,

16 For the voice of him that reproacheth and blasphemeth; by reason of the enemy and avenger.

17 All this is come upon us; yet have we not forgotten thee, neither have we dealt falsely in thy covenant.

18 Our heart is not turned back, neither have our steps declined from thy way;

19 Though thou hast sore broken us in the place of dragons, and covered us with the shadow of death.

20 If we have forgotten the name of our God, or stretched out our hands to a strange god;

21 Shall not God search this out? for he knoweth the secrets of the heart.

22 Yea, for thy sake are we killed all the day long; we are counted as sheep for the slaughter.

23 Awake, why sleepest thou, O Lord? Arise, cast us not off for ever.

24 Wherefore hidest thou thy face, and forgettest our affliction and our oppression?

25 For our soul is bowed down to the dust: our belly cleaveth unto the earth.

26 Arise for our help, and redeem us for thy mercies' sake.

—*King James Bible*

Psalm 70

1 Make haste, O God, to deliver me; make haste to help me, O Lord.

2 Let them be ashamed and confounded that seek after my soul: let them be turned backward, and put to confusion, that desire my hurt.

3 Let them be turned back for a reward of their shame that say, Aha, aha.

4 Let all those that seek thee rejoice and be glad in thee: and let such as love thy salvation say continually, Let God be magnified.

5 But I am poor and needy: make haste unto me, O God: thou art my help and my deliverer; O Lord, make no tarrying.

—*King James Bible*

Psalm 119

1 Blessed are the undefiled in the way, who walk in the law of the Lord.

2 Blessed are they that keep his testimonies, and that seek him with the whole heart.

3 They also do no iniquity: they walk in his ways.

4 Thou hast commanded us to keep thy precepts diligently.

5 O that my ways were directed to keep thy statutes!

6 Then shall I not be ashamed, when I have respect unto all thy commandments.

7 I will praise thee with uprightness of heart, when I shall have learned thy righteous judgments.

8 I will keep thy statutes: O forsake me not utterly.

9 Wherewithal shall a young man cleanse his way? by taking heed thereto according to thy word.

10 With my whole heart have I sought thee: O let me not wander from thy commandments.

11 Thy word have I hid in mine heart, that I might not sin against thee.

12 Blessed art thou, O Lord: teach me thy statutes.

13 With my lips have I declared all the judgments of thy mouth.

14 I have rejoiced in the way of thy testimonies, as much as in all riches.

15 I will meditate in thy precepts, and have respect unto thy ways.

16 I will delight myself in thy statutes: I will not forget thy word.

17 Deal bountifully with thy servant, that I may live, and keep thy word.

18 Open thou mine eyes, that I may behold wondrous things out of thy law.

19 I am a stranger in the earth: hide not thy commandments from me.

20 My soul breaketh for the longing that it hath unto thy judgments at all times.

21 Thou hast rebuked the proud that are cursed, which do err from thy commandments.

22 Remove from me reproach and contempt; for I have kept thy testimonies.

23 Princes also did sit and speak against me: but thy servant did meditate in thy statutes.

24 Thy testimonies also are my delight and my counselors.

25 My soul cleaveth unto the dust: quicken thou me according to thy word.

26 I have declared my ways, and thou heardest me: teach me thy statutes.

27 Make me to understand the way of thy precepts: so shall I talk of thy wondrous works.

28 My soul melteth for heaviness: strengthen thou me according unto thy word.

29 Remove from me the way of lying: and grant me thy law graciously.

30 I have chosen the way of truth: thy judgments have I laid before me.

31 I have stuck unto thy testimonies: O Lord, put me not to shame.

32 I will run the way of thy commandments, when thou shalt enlarge my heart.

33 Teach me, O Lord, the way of thy statutes; and I shall keep it unto the end.

34 Give me understanding, and I shall keep thy law; yea, I shall observe it with my whole heart.

35 Make me to go in the path of thy commandments; for therein do I delight.

36 Incline my heart unto thy testimonies, and not to covetousness.

37 Turn away mine eyes from beholding vanity; and quicken thou me in thy way.

38 Stabilize thy word unto thy servant, who is devoted to thy fear.

39 Turn away my reproach which I fear: for thy judgments are good.

40 Behold, I have longed after thy precepts: quicken me in thy righteousness.

41 Let thy mercies come also unto me, O Lord, even thy salvation, according to thy word.

42 So shall I have wherewith to answer him that reproacheth me: for I trust in thy word.

43 And take not the word of truth utterly out of my mouth; for I have hoped in thy judgments.

44 So shall I keep thy law continually for ever and ever.

45 And I will walk at liberty: for I seek thy precepts.

46 I will speak of thy testimonies also before kings, and will not be ashamed.

47 And I will delight myself in thy commandments, which I have loved.

48 My hands also will I lift up unto thy commandments, which I have loved; and I will meditate in thy statutes.

49 Remember the word unto thy servant, upon which thou hast caused me to hope.

50 This is my comfort in my affliction: for thy word hath quickened me.

51 The proud have had me greatly in derision: yet have I not declined from thy law.

52 I remembered thy judgments of old, O Lord; and have comforted myself.

53 Horror hath taken hold upon me because of the wicked that forsake thy law.

54 Thy statutes have been my songs in the house of my pilgrimage.

55 I have remembered thy name, O Lord, in the night, and have kept thy law.

56 This I had, because I kept thy precepts.

57 Thou art my portion, O Lord: I have said that I would keep thy words.

58 I intreated thy favour with my whole heart: be merciful unto me according to thy word.

59 I thought on my ways, and turned my feet unto thy testimonies.

60 I made haste, and delayed not to keep thy commandments.

61 The bands of the wicked have robbed me: but I have not forgotten thy law.

62 At midnight I will rise to give thanks unto thee because of thy righteous judgments.

63 I am a companion of all them that fear thee, and of them that keep thy precepts.

64 The earth, O Lord, is full of thy mercy: teach me thy statutes.

65 Thou hast dealt well with thy servant, O Lord, according unto thy word.

66 Teach me good judgment and knowledge: for I have believed thy commandments.

67 Before I was afflicted I went astray: but now have I kept thy word.

68 Thou art good, and doest good; teach me thy statutes.

69 The proud have forged a lie against me: but I will keep thy precepts with my whole heart.

70 Their heart is as fat as grease; but I delight in thy law.

71 It is good for me that I have been afflicted; that I might learn thy statutes.

72 The law of thy mouth is better unto me than thousands of gold and silver.

73 Thy hands have made me and fashioned me: give me understanding, that I may learn thy commandments.

74 They that fear thee will be glad when they see me; because I have hoped in thy word.

75 I know, O Lord, that thy judgments are right, and that thou in faithfulness hast afflicted me.

76 Let, I pray thee, thy merciful kindness be for my comfort, according to thy word unto thy servant.

77 Let thy tender mercies come unto me, that I may live: for thy law is my delight.

78 Let the proud be ashamed; for they dealt perversely with me without a cause: but I will meditate in thy precepts.

79 Let those that fear thee turn unto me, and those that have known thy testimonies.

80 Let my heart be sound in thy statutes; that I be not ashamed.

81 My soul fainteth for thy salvation: but I hope in thy word.

82 Mine eyes fail for thy word, saying, When wilt thou comfort me?

83 For I am become like a bottle in the smoke; yet do I not forget thy statutes.

84 How many are the days of thy servant? when wilt thou execute judgment on them that persecute me?

85 The proud have digged pits for me, which are not after thy law.

86 All thy commandments are faithful: they persecute me wrongfully; help thou me.

87 They had almost consumed me upon earth; but I forsook not thy precepts.

88 Quicken me after thy lovingkindness; so shall I keep the testimony of thy mouth.

89 For ever, O Lord, thy word is settled in heaven.

90 Thy faithfulness is unto all generations: thou hast established the earth, and it abideth.

91 They continue this day according to thine ordinances: for all are thy servants.

92 Unless thy law had been my delights, I should then have perished in mine affliction.

93 I will never forget thy precepts: for with them thou hast quickened me.

94 I am thine, save me: for I have sought thy precepts.

95 The wicked have waited for me to destroy me: but I will consider thy testimonies.

96 I have seen an end of all perfection: but thy commandment is exceeding broad.

97 O how love I thy law! it is my meditation all the day.

98 Thou through thy commandments hast made me wiser than mine enemies: for they are ever with me.

99 I have more understanding than all my teachers: for thy testimonies are my meditation.

100 I understand more than the ancients, because I keep thy precepts.

101 I have refrained my feet from every evil way, that I might keep thy word.

102 I have not departed from thy judgments: for thou hast taught me.

103 How sweet are thy words unto my taste! yea, sweeter than honey to my mouth!

104 Through thy precepts I get understanding: therefore I hate every false way.

105 Thy word is a lamp unto my feet, and a light unto my path.

106 I have sworn, and I will perform it, that I will keep thy righteous judgments.

107 I am afflicted very much: quicken me, O Lord, according unto thy word.

108 Accept, I beseech thee, the freewill offerings of my mouth, O Lord, and teach me thy judgments.

109 My soul is continually in my hand: yet do I not forget thy law.

110 The wicked have laid a snare for me: yet I erred not from thy precepts.

111 Thy testimonies have I taken as an heritage for ever: for they are the rejoicing of my heart.

112 I have inclined mine heart to perform thy statutes always, even unto the end.

113 I hate vain thoughts: but thy law do I love.

114 Thou art my hiding place and my shield: I hope in thy word.

115 Depart from me, ye evildoers: for I will keep the commandments of my God.

116 Uphold me according unto thy word, that I may live: and let me not be ashamed of my hope.

117 Hold thou me up, and I shall be safe: and I will have respect unto thy statutes continually.

118 Thou hast trodden down all them that err from thy statutes: for their deceit is falsehood.

119 Thou puttest away all the wicked of the earth like dross: therefore I love thy testimonies.

120 My flesh trembleth for fear of thee; and I am afraid of thy judgments.

121 I have done judgment and justice: leave me not to mine oppressors.

122 Be surety for thy servant for good: let not the proud oppress me.

123 Mine eyes fail for thy salvation, and for the word of thy righteousness.

124 Deal with thy servant according unto thy mercy, and teach me thy statutes.

125 I am thy servant; give me understanding, that I may know thy testimonies.

126 It is time for thee, Lord, to work: for they have made void thy law.

127 Therefore I love thy commandments above gold; yea, above fine gold.

128 Therefore I esteem all thy precepts concerning all things to be right; and I hate every false way.

129 Thy testimonies are wonderful: therefore doth my soul keep them.

130 The entrance of thy words giveth light; it giveth understanding unto the simple.

131 I opened my mouth, and panted: for I longed for thy commandments.

132 Look thou upon me, and be merciful unto me, as thou usest to do unto those that love thy name.

133 Order my steps in thy word: and let not any iniquity have dominion over me.

134 Deliver me from the oppression of man: so will I keep thy precepts.

135 Make thy face to shine upon thy servant; and teach me thy statutes.

136 Rivers of waters run down mine eyes, because they keep not thy law.

137 Righteous art thou, O Lord, and upright are thy judgments.

138 Thy testimonies that thou hast commanded are righteous and very faithful.

139 My zeal hath consumed me, because mine enemies have forgotten thy words.

140 Thy word is very pure: therefore thy servant loveth it.

141 I am small and despised: yet do not I forget thy precepts.

142 Thy righteousness is an everlasting righteousness, and thy law is the truth.

143 Trouble and anguish have taken hold on me: yet thy commandments are my delights.

144 The righteousness of thy testimonies is everlasting: give me understanding, and I shall live.

145 I cried with my whole heart; hear me, O Lord: I will keep thy statutes.

146 I cried unto thee; save me, and I shall keep thy testimonies.

147 I prevented the dawning of the morning, and cried: I hoped in thy word.

148 Mine eyes prevent the night watches, that I might meditate in thy word.

149 Hear my voice according unto thy lovingkindness: O Lord, quicken me according to thy judgment.

150 They draw nigh that follow after mischief: they are far from thy law.

151 Thou art near, O Lord; and all thy commandments are truth.

152 Concerning thy testimonies, I have known of old that thou hast founded them for ever.

153 Consider mine affliction, and deliver me: for I do not forget thy law.

154 Plead my cause, and deliver me: quicken me according to thy word.

155 Salvation is far from the wicked: for they seek not thy statutes.

156 Great are thy tender mercies, O Lord: quicken me according to thy judgments.

157 Many are my persecutors and mine enemies; yet do I not decline from thy testimonies.

158 I beheld the transgressors, and was grieved; because they kept not thy word.

159 Consider how I love thy precepts: quicken me, O Lord, according to thy lovingkindness.

160 Thy word is true from the beginning: and every one of thy righteous judgments endureth for ever.

161 Princes have persecuted me without a cause: but my heart standeth in awe of thy word.

162 I rejoice at thy word, as one that findeth great spoil.

163 I hate and abhor lying: but thy law do I love.

164 Seven times a day do I praise thee because of thy righteous judgments.

165 Great peace have they which love thy law: and nothing shall offend them.

166 Lord, I have hoped for thy salvation, and done thy commandments.

167 My soul hath kept thy testimonies; and I love them exceedingly.

168 I have kept thy precepts and thy testimonies: for all my ways are before thee.

169 Let my cry come near before thee, O Lord: give me understanding according to thy word.

170 Let my supplication come before thee: deliver me according to thy word.

171 My lips shall utter praise, when thou hast taught me thy statutes.

172 My tongue shall speak of thy word: for all thy commandments are righteousness.

173 Let thine hand help me; for I have chosen thy precepts.

174 I have longed for thy salvation, O Lord; and thy law is my delight.

175 Let my soul live, and it shall praise thee; and let thy judgments help me.

176 I have gone astray like a lost sheep; seek thy servant; for I do not forget thy commandments.

—*King James Bible*

Psalm 133

1 Behold, how good and how pleasant it is for brethren to dwell together in unity!

2 It is like the precious ointment upon the head, that ran down upon the beard, even Aaron's beard: that went down to the skirts of his garments;

3 As the dew of Hermon, and as the dew that descended upon the mountains of Zion: for there the Lord commanded the blessing, even life for evermore.

—*King James Bible*

Psalm 148

1 Praise ye the Lord. Praise ye the Lord from the heavens: praise him in the heights.

2 Praise ye him, all his angels: praise ye him, all his hosts.

3 Praise ye him, sun and moon: praise him, all ye stars of light.

4 Praise him, ye heavens of heavens, and ye waters that be above the heavens.

5 Let them praise the name of the Lord: for he commanded, and they were created.

6 He hath also established them for ever and ever: he hath made a decree which shall not pass.

7 Praise the Lord from the earth, ye dragons, and all deeps:

8 Fire, and hail; snow, and vapors; stormy wind fulfilling his word:

9 Mountains, and all hills; fruitful trees, and all cedars:

10 Beasts, and all cattle; creeping things, and flying fowl:

11 Kings of the earth, and all people; princes, and all judges of the earth:

12 Both young men, and maidens; old men, and children:

13 Let them praise the name of the Lord: for his name alone is excellent; his glory is above the earth and heaven.

14 He also exalteth the horn of his people, the praise of all his saints; even of the children of Israel, a people near unto him. Praise ye the Lord.

—*King James Bible*

RECOMMENDED READING

The spells, rituals, and rites contained in this book are based on a lifetime of practice, initiation, and research. If you would like to continue your own readings and research in the areas of love magic and spirituality, the following list is a great place to start your journey.

Books

Dorsey, Lilith. *Voodoo and Afro-Caribbean Paganism*. New York, NY: Citadel Press, 2005. My comprehensive work about all different variations of African Traditional religion. You will find more spells here and a deeper understanding of the Lwa, Orisha, and other energies of the universe. A good book for both beginners and experts alike.

Duquette, Lon Milo. *Understanding Aleister Crowley's Thoth Tarot*. San Francisco, CA: Weiser Books, 2003. This work helps you better understand Crowley. It includes an in-depth look at the tarot suits and how they are relevant in context. There is also information on the Tree of Life and how it relates to the tarot.

Illes, Judika. *Magic When You Need It: 150 Spells You Can't Live Without*. San Francisco, CA: Weiser Books, 2008. Just like the title says, this book covers the essential spells needed for every witchy person's magic bag of tricks. Expand your personal grimoire with this important book.

Jodorowsky, Alejandro. *Psychomagic*. Rochester, VT: Inner Traditions, 2010. To those who are familiar with his work, Jodorowsky is an iconoclast of mythic proportions who is worthy of his nickname "Maestro." Among occult circles, he is famous for his work with tarot, but in reality his work in this area is so much more. He developed an entire system called "Psychomagic," which is explored in this book.

I highly recommend it for anyone wishing to access and explore their higher selves. He provides unique and creative solutions for exploring these realms that allow individuals to expand their minds, and this is where the magic truly happens.

Kaldera, Raven, and Tannin Schwartzstein. *Handfasting and Wedding Rituals*. St. Paul, MN: Llewellyn Publications, 2003. This is one of the most comprehensive and complete texts about pagan weddings and handfastings. Schwartzstein is one of the most knowledgeable writers I know, and this book is full of rituals for every type of wedding, including nontraditional and interfaith ceremonies.

Linden, Mishlen (ed.). *Women of Babalon: A Howling of Women's Voices*. New Orleans, LA: Black Moon Publishing, 2015. A collection of writings about sex, love, and possession from thirteen of the most powerful female occultists, including myself. It speaks to direct ecstatic experience with the God or Goddess, and how this manifests in all its sensual glory.

Martinie, Louis, and Sallie Ann Glassman. *The New Orleans Voodoo Tarot*. Rochester, VT: Destiny Books, 1992. I have been a professional tarot reader for over two decades and this is my favorite deck, and that of my clients too, hands down. Ms. Glassman's haunting images artfully complement my dear friend Louis's insightful words. It makes a great starter deck, or it can simply be used as a tool for discovering more about the exciting world of New Orleans Voodoo.

Morrison, Dorothy. *Utterly Wicked*. St. Louis, MO: Willow Tree Press, 2007. Have a difficult problem in your love life that you need to get rid of fast? Then this is the book for you. It details almost every curse, hex, or the like for removing hindrances from your path. Ms. Morrison is an effective, practical, and amusing witch, and this comes across in all her writings.

Rigaud, Milo. *Ve-Ve: Ritual Voodoo Diagrams*. New York, NY: French and European Publications, 1974. Rigaud set the standard for Afro-Caribbean scholarship in the 1930s and '40s with his comprehensive works about Haitian Vodou. Throughout this book you're reading, I mention using veves as part of love spells; this Rigaud book contains a wide variety of them, over five hundred pages.

Riley, Jana. *Tarot Dictionary and Compendium*. York Beach, ME: Samuel Weiser, 1995. Every divination library should include this book. Riley has taken the time and care to compile a comprehensive guide to many different tarot decks, meanings, and interpretations. Many tarot readers will tell you that you need to throw away the book; I believe you should do that only after you have read it first. This book, which is actually several different takes on tarot, gives you a great starting point for understanding the way this ancient system of divination operates.

Telesco, Patricia, and Don Waterhawk. *Sacred Beat: From the Heart of the Drum Circle*. Boston, MA: Red Wheel/Weiser Books, 2003. For many pagans, old and new, they feel their truest and most authentic self around the fire at a Sacred Drum Circle. This book explores the primal root of this phenomenon from a drummer's and a dancer's perspective.

About the Author

Lilith Dorsey, MA is a magical practitioner and Voodoo priestess with initiation and training in several traditions, including Celtic, Afro-Caribbean (Santeria, Voodoo, and Vodun), and Native American spiritualities. Lilith has been a dancer and choreographer with Dr. John's Night Tripper Voodoo show. She is editor/publisher of *Oshun-African Magickal Quarterly* and the author of *Voodoo and Afro-Caribbean Paganism.*

To Our Readers

Weiser Books, an imprint of Red Wheel/Weiser, publishes books across the entire spectrum of occult, esoteric, speculative, and New Age subjects. Our mission is to publish quality books that will make a difference in people's lives without advocating any one particular path or field of study. We value the integrity, originality, and depth of knowledge of our authors.

Our readers are our most important resource, and we appreciate your input, suggestions, and ideas about what you would like to see published.

Visit our website at *www.redwheelweiser.com* to learn about our upcoming books and free downloads, and be sure to go to *www.redwheelweiser.com/ newsletter* to sign up for newsletters and exclusive offers.

You can also contact us at *info@rwwbooks.com* or at

Red Wheel/Weiser, LLC
65 Parker Street, Suite 7
Newburyport, MA 01950